The Parson's Handbook

Percy Dearmer

THE

PARSON'S HANDBOOK

CONTAINING PRACTICAL DIRECTIONS BOTH FOR PARSONS
AND OTHERS AS TO THE MANAGEMENT OF THE PARISH
CHURCH AND ITS SERVICE ACCORDING TO

THE ENGLISH USE

AS SET FORTH IN THE BOOK OF COMMON PRAYER

WITH AN INTRODUCTORY ESSAY ON CONFORMITY TO THE
CHURCH OF ENGLAND

BY THE REV.

PERCY DEARMER, M.A.

1899

CONTENTS

INTRODUCTION

The object of this Handbook is to help, in however humble a way, towards remedying the lamentable confusion, lawlessness, and vulgarity which are conspicuous in the Church at this time.

1. The confusion is due to the want of liturgical knowledge among the clergy, and of consistent example among those in authority. Some years ago it was natural and inevitable; but at the present day it has no right to exist. For a number of diligent scholars and liturgical experts have settled the main points beyond reasonable dispute. All that is wanted is for that knowledge to be disseminated; and it is with this object that the present Handbook is put forth, by one whose only claim to consideration is that he has attempted to popularise the conclusions of those far more conversant with the matter than himself.

2. The lawlessness is due to more complex causes. It is not confined, as is popularly supposed, to the 'advanced' clergy. Indeed it is even greater among those who are called 'moderate' and among those who dislike all ceremonial. Among all classes its ultimate cause is that congregationalist spirit which has been the inevitable outcome of a period of transition and confusion. Among those who dislike ceremonial, the lawlessness is due to a conservatism which prefers late Hanoverian traditions to the plain words of the Prayer Book,-— an unfortunate position, both because those traditions belong to a period of exceptional sloth and worldliness, and also because the date of the Prayer Book makes it impossible for us to read it aright if we try to do so through Hanoverian spectacles. Wesley and the Oxford Methodists, who started the noble Evangelical revival, did not fall into this error; and, indeed, the very name of 'Methodist' (which meant what 'Ritualist' in its popular sense now means) was given to them because of their care in following the fasts and other observances of the Church.

The lawlessness of those at the other extreme, who are commonly called Ritualists (would that they always deserved the name!), was brought about by the troubles of the days of litigation. Their object at first was the very reverse of lawlessness: they wished only to obey the Prayer Book in all its rubrics. But, unfortunately, the prelates of those days were not conversant with the subject, and were not prepared to obey the Prayer Book. They allowed their clergy to be prosecuted by unconstitutional courts that did not scruple to insert the word 'not' into the Ornaments Rubric; they contented themselves with inveighing against such things as the use of the surplice in the pulpit, an essentially unimportant custom, which had been largely practised in the days of Queen Anne, and has now been eagerly adopted by the Evangelical clergy. Consequently the 'ritualistic' clergy were forced, in the interests of obedience to the Prayer Book, to disobey the Bishops. From that grew up unconsciously a spirit of confirmed lawlessness; and many of those who began by taking their stand on the Ornaments Rubric, ended by denying it in favour of the customs of a very hostile foreign Church; till they seemed almost to agree with their former opponents that such ornaments as were in this Church of England in the second year of Edward VI. should not be in use to-day; and some of them seemed to prefer to the liturgical forms 'in the said Book prescribed' those forms which the Book had rather proscribed.

The lawlessness of those in the middle or 'moderate 'section has been due to that excellent spirit of compromise, which, however, if it be not rightly used, ends in a mere combination of the errors of both extremes. As it is not generally understood that in 'moderate' churches the Prayer Book is largely disobeyed, one instance may here be given. The sermon is ordered in the Prayer Book to be preached at the Communion Service; and yet in churches of this description it is preached at Mattins, and thus the service which we get from the Bible is pushed on one side in favour of the service which we get from the monks. In the case of the Bishops and Cathedral dignitaries this lawlessness is aggravated by the fact that our own Canons order them specially to use the cope and the proper vestments for gospeller and epistler.

Recently, however, there has been a general move towards a more legitimate position. On the one hand, many of the Bishops have begun to accept the directions of the Prayer Book and Canons. On the other hand, many of the clergy have come to realise, with something of a shock, the untenable position into which they had drifted; and on all hands there is an openly-expressed readiness to obey lawful authority. This renewal of the spirit of Catholic obedience is of the happiest augury for the Church of England. It is in the hope that this Handbook may be able to assist in its practice that I am putting it forward at this time.

3. The vulgarity in the Church is due to less serious causes; but is none the less serious in its effects. One who has spent much of his life among those who earn their living by writing and drawing may

be allowed to assert that the alienation of these, perhaps the most influential classes in modern society, is one of the most startling facts that are before us. What it has already led to in France is obvious to every enquirer. How far it has already gone in England the tone of our newspapers shows. I have pointed out elsewhere that, did the Guild of St. Luke consist of that other profession of which the Saint is patron, there would not be a dozen men present at the annual service in St. Paul's, instead of the immense crowd of medical men who now assemble there. It is not now science but art that is out of touch with religion. The doctors would not be there if the clergy had for the last fifty years steadily supported quackery, and refused to recognise the great advances made in medical science. This is exactly what has happened in the case of art. The clergy have worked on purely commercial lines; they are mostly even now content with decoration that is the ridicule of competent artists, or is ignored by them as not being even amusing; and the Church has almost entirely failed to call to her service the great artists and craftsmen of which the last generation produced so large a number. Her place as patroness of art has been taken by the merchants of Birmingham, Manchester, and Liverpool.

I acknowledge that the failure to retain these classes of brain-workers has been also due to other causes which are outside the province of this book-to our sermons, for instance. Yet it must be remembered that our Church is still the most learned Church in Christendom; and also that a want of grip of modern thought is as much shown in art as in anything else. In the case of music, which is in a more fortunate position than the other arts, it is recognised that those churches where the music is bad drive away people with sensitive ears. It is not recognised that people with sensitive eyes are driven away by the excruciating faults from which very few indeed of our churches are free. And there is another class of persons concerned, the largest of all, the working class. For vulgarity in the long-run always means cheapness, and cheapness means the tyranny of the sweater. It has been pointed out that a modern preacher often stands in a sweated pulpit, wearing a sweated surplice over a suit of clothes that were not produced under fair conditions, and, holding a sweated book in one hand, with the other he points to the machine-made cross at the jerry-built altar, and appeals to the sacred principles of mutual sacrifice and love.

This vulgarity is due to much the same causes as the confusion and lawlessness of which I have already spoken. It is due to a failure to recognise the principle of authority; and authority is as necessary in art as it is in religion. Every one does what is right in his own eyes, because we have failed to recognise the first principles of the matter, the necessity of wholesome tradition on the one hand and of due deference to the artist's judgment on the other. We do not listen to the artist when he tells us about art, and we are surprised that he does not listen to us when we tell him about religion. It is partly in the hope that this Handbook may help in restoring the ancient spirit of beauty in our churches that I venture to put it forward.

Fortunately our Church, in its wise persistent conservatism, refers us for our standard to a definite period of twelve months, in the loyal adoption of which standard both confusion and vulgarity would be as impossible as lawlessness. Much of the tawdry stupidity of our churches is due to the decline of art subsequent to that date, and to the senseless imitation of those meretricious ornaments, both of the Church and its Ministers, with which ignorant and indiscreet persons have ruined the ancient beauty of Roman Catholic churches. We who loyally obey the Prayer Book are mercifully saved from the possibility of that barbarous degradation, which educated Frenchmen and Italians despise and regret not less than ourselves.

The cure, therefore, for all our troubles and deficiencies is to practise that loyal obedience to lawful authority which the clergy have sworn to do in the solemn declaration of the amended Canon 36:—

' I A. B. do solemnly make the following declaration: I assent to the thirty-nine Articles of Religion, and to the Book of Common Prayer, and of the Ordering of Bishops, Priests, and Deacons. I believe the doctrine of the Church of England, as therein set forth, to be agreeable to the Word of God; and in public prayer and administration of the Sacraments I will use the Form in the said Book prescribed, and none other, except so far as shall be ordered by lawful authority.'

The Archbishop of Canterbury, in a recent charge at Maidstone, has pointed out that, though the Church of England wisely allows a certain amount of doctrinal latitude to her clergy, she is very strict as to ceremonial. The Declaration supports this statement; nothing more enthusiastic than 'assent' is required to the Articles, but the undertaking as to the forms of public prayer admits of no compromise.

Is there then any excuse for laxity in the conduct of public prayer and the administration of the Sacraments? Clearly not. Yet the popular idea is that the English Church is 'comprehensive,' and that its services can with equal loyalty be conducted in an infinite variety of ways; they can be 'low,' or 'of a cathedral type,' or 'high,' or even, strange as it may seem, 'Roman.' But this the Archbishop has shown to be, like so many other popular ideas, a fallacy. The Church is comprehensive, but only on the doctrinal side. 'It is the unity of ceremonial that makes the toleration of diversity of opinion possible. The ceremonial stands before us as the order of the Church. The teaching is, and must be to a very large extent, the voice of the individual. The ceremonial is for all alike.'

Yet, no doubt, the Archbishop himself would allow a certain toleration of disobedience, even in ceremonial; for we live in a time of transition when the rigid use of authority would be disastrous, and even unjust. Those who disobey, for instance, the Ornaments Rubric, or those Canons upon which the Archbishop based his claim for obedience, he would yet, I imagine, allow to continue in their laxity, both for the sake of peace and a true far-reaching justice, and because, when an acknowledged duty has been in abeyance for centuries, the revival of its claim must necessarily be gradual and tender. The obedience, therefore, with which we are concerned at the present time is a voluntary obedience. We are impelled, not by a Star Chamber but by Conscience, to obey. We are put upon our honour to conform to the Prayer Book as completely as we can; and even school-boys know that obedience under these conditions is that which must be most thoroughly, most loyally, and most honourably given.

The Church of England, then, is not that flaccid thing which some seem to suppose. She 'has a mind of her own; a mind, and therewith a character, a temperament, a complexion; and of this mind the Prayer Book is the main and representative expression.'[1]

How are we to discover that mind, how are we to carry out that unity of ceremonial which stands before us as the order of the Church? It is not, I think, difficult if we go straight to the Prayer Book.

1. 'The Church,' says our Twentieth Article, 'hath power to decree rites or ceremonies,' but not 'to ordain anything that is contrary to God's Word written,' nor 'to decree anything against the same.'[2] As a preliminary, then, the mind of the Church is to be sought in the Bible upon which it is based.

Now it is certain that the worship described both in the Old and New Testaments is what is called 'ritualistic.' The minute directions as to the ornaments and vestments of the ministers are familiar to every reader of the Pentateuch; and these directions go even into such detail as the proper ingredients of incense[3] Nor is there any hint that this ritualism was to be dropped under the New Covenant, as is sometimes gratuitously assumed. Our Lord attended the ritualistic services of the Temple; nay, He was careful to be present at those great feasts when the ceremonial was most elaborate. Yet no word of censure ever escaped His lips. This was the more remarkable, because He was evidently far from ignoring the subject. No one ever appreciated the danger of formalism so keenly as He: He did condemn most strongly the vain private ceremonies of the Pharisees. Also, on two occasions He cleansed the Temple, driving out, not those who adorned it with ceremonial, but those who dishonoured it with commercialism. That is to say, His only interference with the ritualistic worship of the Temple was to secure it against profane interruption.

The use of incense is a good test as to the continuance of ceremonial under the New Covenant; because it is now regarded, even by some Bishops, as a mark of extreme ritualism. Its use is mentioned in the last prophetic book of the Old Testament[4] as one of the signs of the New Covenant. The birth of the Fore-runner was announced to his father when 'his lot was to burn incense,'[5] a singularly inopportune moment from the Puritan point of view. One of the three significant gifts offered to our Lord at His birth was incense.[6] In the Revelation an account is given of the ideal worship of the redeemed, by one who, more than any other man, had opportunities of knowing our Lord's mind upon the subject. Now the worship he describes is again ritualistic; and the use of no less than twenty-eight 'bowls' of incense is mentioned.[7] It is mentioned again three chapters further on[8] in a manner that is significant; for it is then used ceremonially at the altar. The angel stands 'at (or over) the altar, having a golden censer,' he is given 'much incense,' to 'add it unto the prayers of all the saints upon the golden altar.' 'And the smoke of the incense, with (or for) the prayers of the saints, went up before God out of the angel's hand.' The Sarum Missal itself hardly gives a more complete description of the ceremonial use of incense.

2. The next step towards arriving at the mind of the English Church is to read the Title-page of the Prayer Book, where, if anywhere, one might expect to find a succinct description of its contents. As a matter of fact we do find such a description:—

The Book of
Common Prayer
and administration of
The Sacraments
and other
Rites and Ceremonies of the Church
According to the Use of
The Church of England.

It is no new manual, then, of Protestant devotions, to be carried out in some new-fangled way, but it contains the ordinary services of the Catholic Church, of which the Church of England is a part. In accordance with the ancient right of each national Church—even of each diocese—to frame its own 'use' of these Catholic rites and ceremonies, the Prayer Book hereby establishes the English Use.

3. This takes us one step farther, to the prefaces of the Prayer Book. The first of these, *'The Preface,'* is the latest in point of time, having been written in 1661; and it is the least important, being mainly taken up with a refutation of Puritan objections. It gives excellent reasons for the last revision,[9] mentioning among other improvements those made 'for the better direction' of the clergy, 'in the Calendars and Rubricks,' which improvements, it is well known, all emphasised the Catholic character of our services. Referring to some of the Puritan proposals it incidentally repeats the claim we have already noticed in the title-page; these proposals it accuses of 'secretly striking at some established doctrine, or laudable practice of the Church of England, or indeed of the whole Catholick Church of Christ.'

Far more important are the next two prefaces, which are taken from the First Prayer Book of 1549. The first, *'Concerning the Service of the Church,'* is an adaptation of that to the reformed Breviary of Cardinal Quignon, which it follows in all essentials. This model, which the English Church thought the best for that of the introduction to its Book of Common Prayer, was published by authority of Pope Clement VII. in 1535. Nothing could more clearly show the Catholic idea which the compilers of our Prayer Book had of the meaning of the word 'reformed.' The words of the preface make this point still clearer. It is not concerned with sacraments or ceremonial, but throughout only with the practical question of restoring the lectionary and psalter to its ancient thoroughness and simplicity in accordance with the 'godly and decent order of the ancient Fathers.' Four times in this short preface is the authority of these 'ancient Fathers' invoked. In accordance with their example the language is to be that which is understood; untrue, uncertain, and superstitious readings are to be dropped, and nothing to be read that is not in Scripture, or 'agreeable to the same.' This is the most important of our prefaces, because it stood alone at the head of the First Prayer Book, and it has been with us ever since. If Cranmer meant that Book to lead to Protestant practices, he certainly concealed his purpose remarkably well.[10]

This preface concludes with a reference to the Bishop, which it is important to notice at the present time. The Bishop of the diocese (and, failing him, the Archbishop) is to 'take order for the quieting and appeasing of any 'doubts' that may arise, but only 'so that the same order be not contrary to anything contained in this Book.' He is the servant of the Church, not its master, the administrator of its ritual, not its maker. The same principle appears in the 74th Canon, of Decency of Apparel,—'We therefore, following their ["the ancient and flourishing Churches of Christ"] grave judgment, and the ancient custom of the Church of England, and hoping that in time newfangledness in apparel[11] in some factious persons will die of itself, do constitute and appoint, that the Archbishops and Bishops shall not intermit to use the accustomed apparel of their degrees.'

The third preface, 'Of Ceremonies, why some be retained, and some abolished,' is also probably by Cranmer. In the First Book it was placed at the end,[12] and was followed by 'certain notes' which ordered the use of certain vestments to be mentioned later, and, after the example of the old Missals, allowed of the omission of the Gloria, Creed, etc. on some occasions. The ceremonies it speaks of as abolished could not, at least, be the use of those vestments, nor such things as Unction and Mass for the dead, which were ordered in that Book; nor those which were allowed in that Book,[13] 'kneeling, crossing, holding up of the hands, knocking upon the breast, and other gestures.'

What ceremonies, then, were abolished? Clearly, it could be only those which were abolished by the authority of the Church. Mr. Perry long ago pointed out that those characteristic acts of Tudor tyranny, the Injunctions of Henry, Edward, Mary, and Elizabeth, 'were grounded on the ecclesiastical supremacy of the Crown, a prerogative which did not in reality confer upon the sovereign a right to make laws for the Church, and which was not even by authority of Parliament.' As to what ceremonies were abolished the preface is studiously vague. There is no hint of any revolutionary change in ritual, though there is a wholesome reminder of the fact that 'Christ's Gospel is not a ceremonial law.' It is assumed throughout that only those ceremonies have been changed which the rubrics of the Book explicitly claim to have changed.

And it was not ritualism, nor beauty, nor symbolism, that was abolished, but certain ceremonies, some of which, indeed, at the first were of godly intent and purpose devised, 'but had at length turned to vanity and superstition.' It is precisely, by the way, for these reasons that practices have been over and over again abolished in the Roman Church itself, where yet indiscreet devotion' still works such havoc. Some, by 'the great excess and multitude of them,' had become an intolerable burden; but the 'most weighty cause of the abolishment of certain ceremonies was that they had been so far abused' by the 'superstitious blindness' of the ignorant and the 'unsatiable avarice' of those who traded on it, 'that the abuses could not well be taken away, the thing remaining still.' So, then, even those ceremonies which have been abolished were of godly intent originally, or at the worst due to undiscreet devotion and a zeal without knowledge, and were not removed for their own sake, but because of certain abuses which had fastened inseparably upon them.

This does not look much like a destruction of ritualism. Yet even this is further safeguarded in the next paragraph, by a cutting reply to those who wanted 'innovations and newfangledness'—'surely when the old may be well used, then they cannot reasonably reprove the old only for their age, without bewraying of their own folly.' Indeed so conservative is this preface that it does not hesitate to declare that innovations (' as much as may be with true setting forth of Christ's religion') are 'always to be eschewed.'

After a happy apology for the retained ceremonies that they are 'neither dark nor dumb,' the preface concludes with the significant declaration that, while we claim our right to an English use, 'we condemn no other nations,' a remark which shows how far the spirit of the Prayer Book is removed from the censorious Protestantism with which we are familiar.[14]

4. From the prefaces the Prayer Book takes us to the Calendar, where we find, as we should expect, a simplification indeed, but a simplification which contains all the main features of the old,—the great feasts, and the seasons, the saints' days (which are broadly classified into two divisions only). Hidden away under the 'Lessons proper for Holy-Days,' as if specially to secure them against Puritan

attacks, we find the old phrase the 'Annunciation of our Lady,' and the old names for the services of 'Mattins' and 'Evensong.' Passing through the Calendar, with its careful provision for a continuous reading of the Holy Bible, we come upon a list of the 'Vigils, Fasts and Days of Abstinence' which are 'to be observed,'[15] as of old time.

From this we come to the rubric as to the 'accustomed place' in which Morning and Evening Prayer are to be said, a rubric that was revised in 1559 by the significant omission of the provision of the Second Book, that the place shall be such, and the Minister shall so turn himself, 'as the people may best hear.' The concluding sentence, however, of the rubric in the Second Book—its one conservative provision— was carefully retained through all revisions—'And the Chancels shall remain as they have done in times past.' No alteration of the pre-Reformation chancel was ordered in the First Book; the former arrangement was ordered to be continued in the Second Book, and each succeeding revision has repeated it *verbatim*. Yet a century ago in vast numbers of churches the chancels, instead of their remaining as in times past, were looked upon as a kind of lumber-room, to be cleared out once a quarter for the administration of the Holy Communion, or else as a place for the erection of select pews for those in goodly apparel to whom (on payment of a consideration) could be said, 'Sit thou here in a good place.'[16] This alone would suffice to show how utterly different were the practices of our grandfathers from the mind of the Church of England.

So far, then, by a plain consideration of the introduction to the Prayer Book we have seen that its 'mind" is steeped in the old ceremonial traditions of the Bible, of the 'ancient Fathers,' and of that which was old in the sense of being the medieval practice up to 1549; that it forbids any ceremonial principles contrary to those of the New Testament; that it refuses to condemn (though it does not sanction) the practices of any other nation; that it claims in the same spirit the old Catholic right to set forward an English use for its own people: that it declares its changes to be mainly necessitated by the use of a dead language, and by the existence of those abuses of avarice and ignorant superstition, which forced the Church to abolish certain ceremonies that in themselves were of godly intent; that it declares its preference, wherever it is possible, for the old as against new-fangled innovations; that it is, in a word, a simplification of that which is primitive and medieval, and not in any sense a creation of a new Protestant ceremonial.

We have seen, further, how it retained the old arrangement of the Church's year, with its fasts and festivals, and the old arrangement of the chancels. That it retained also all that was essential of the old Catholic services was admitted even in the eighteenth century. Indeed the Catholic nature of our 'Popish Liturgy,' as those call it who confuse what is Popish with what is Catholic, has been consistently urged against it by the Puritans, from the days of Thomas Cartwright[17] to the present time.

We have now only to consider the most important point of all, the Ornaments Rubric. This will show us how much of the old ceremonial is to be retained.

5. Some of our documents are studiously vague in their wording. But from such vagueness the Ornaments Rubric is conspicuously free:—

'And here it is to be noted, That such Ornaments of the Church, and of the Ministers thereof, at all times of their Ministration, shall be retained, and be in use, as were in this Church of England, by the authority of Parliament, in the second year of the reign of King Edward the Sixth.'

This is the only direction we have as to what the priest is to wear,[18] and almost the only one as to what he is to use, in the services of the Church. It is our sole authority for the use of organs and lecterns, just as much as for that of censers and roods. We are nowhere else told to wear the surplice any more than the chasuble; for those Canons of 1603 that deal with vestments have been superseded by the re-enactment of this Rubric in 1662, and are only in force because the vestments they order are included in the Rubric.[19] The only reason why the surplice was retained and the chasuble for so long in abeyance is that bishops thought well to enforce obedience to the law in one respect and not in the other. The Ornaments Rubric is in fact the 'interpretation clause of the Prayer Book.' It covers all the rubrics which are to follow. Through it alone can they be obeyed. The only point of difficulty about the Rubric is that it refers back to a certain period, instead of giving a detailed list of the ornaments and vestments to be used. Would it not have been clearer and more unmistakable, it may be objected, had such a list been given? But a very slight knowledge of English history shows that a list of this kind was not possible at any of the three occasions when the rubric was enacted. Until after the last Revision at the Restoration the idea of dissent was unknown. The Puritans were merely non-conforming churchmen, who continued to communicate at their parish churches, and were as much opposed to the idea of schism as the high churchmen themselves. Therefore every effort had to be made to allow them latitude until the fury should be over-past. The bishops found their hands full with trying to enforce the use of the surplice alone, at a time when a large number of the clergy insisted on wearing a cloak, sleeveless jacket, or horseman's coat. So the first two publications of the Rubric (1559 and 1603-4) make a less specific declaration as to vestments than as to ornaments; and the Canons of the latter date were content with requiring copes in cathedral and collegiate churches only, their enforcement being hopelessly impossible in most parish churches. Therefore anything like a list of ornaments would have destroyed the very object for which the Rubric was inserted. Its supporters had to be content to wait for better times.

That they deliberately intended it to mean at least the ornaments used under the First Prayer Book is clear from the character of those who secured its insertion at each revision. In 1559, shortly after Elizabeth's accession, she secured its insertion, 'until other order shall therein be taken,' which order was never taken. She was notoriously in favour of keeping up the old ceremonial, though she was also anxious to avoid offence, and to rally round her the whole people, many of whom had been strongly moved in the Protestant direction by Mary's persecutions.[20] All the alterations, too, of this third Prayer Book were of a markedly Catholic character. In 1604 the Rubric was again inserted. That the exposition of the Sacraments was added to the Catechism at this time, and the Canons issued which enforced the use of copes in cathedrals (in spite of the growing strength of Puritanism and the opposition at the Hampton Court Conference), shows that this second insertion also was deliberately made. In 1662 the Ornaments Rubric was again inserted for the third and last time, with the significant alteration that it was made explicitly to cover the vestments as well as the ornaments of the Church. Its reinsertion was thus very deliberately made, and was accompanied at this time also with changes in the services themselves of a strongly Catholic character. So far from its being inserted carelessly, or from a mere regard for its antiquity, the Puritans formally objected to it at the Savoy Conference—

'Forasmuch as this Rubric seemeth to bring back the Cope, Albe, etc., and other vestments forbidden by the Common Prayer Book, 5 and 6 Edw. vi. [that of 1552, which was cancelled in 1553], and so our reasons alleged against ceremonies under our eighteenth general exception, we desire that it may be wholly left out.'[21]

To this the Bishops replied, 'We think it fit that the Rubric continue as it is.'[22] And they issued it most conspicuously with a page to itself, an arrangement which the printers have tampered with.

Thus, then, the fact that the ornaments had not in fact been 'retained' (for the churches had been spoiled, and the remnants of their ornaments abolished during the Commonwealth[23]) was not regarded as in the least preventing them being revived so that they should be 'in use.' Yet it has been sometimes urged, with more ingenuity than ingenuousness, that we ought not now to use those of the ornaments which became obsolete, because obsolete things cannot be retained. The Revisers deliberately referred back to the year 1548, because they considered that by that year enough had been abolished, and that those ornaments which remained were not incongruous with the reformed service. They must, too, have known that the times were not yet ripe for this complete restoration, for they did not try to enforce more than the former minimum of decency required. They therefore insisted on inserting the Rubric, because they felt the importance of preserving to the Church her ancient heritage of beauty and splendour, and believed that the time would arrive when reason would prevail, and churchmen would come to value their inheritance.

It is almost superfluous to point out the meaning of the various clauses of the Rubric. It was made at the last revision explicitly to order the old vestments as well as ornaments, by the insertion of the words 'and of the Ministers thereof.' Its position before the first prayers in the Book was chosen to give it prominence, and not to confine it to Morning and Evening Prayer; for the ornaments are to be used 'at all times of their Ministration.' These ornaments are not to be retained in the negative sense in which the cope is now retained at Durham or Westminster, but are to 'be in use.' The ornaments to be thus used are not to be affected by any arbitrary acts of Tudor despotism, or of Calvinistic bishops; but are those that were used 'by the authority of Parliament.'[24] And, finally, they are to be those not of modern Rome, nor of medieval Salisbury, nor of the primitive Church, but of 'the second year of King Edward the Sixth.'

The only serious attempt ever made to lessen the effect of this Rubric has been the confining of its meaning to those Ornaments which were mentioned in the First Prayer Book of King Edward vi.; and in support of this it is alleged that Cosin himself (who had a large share in the revision of 1662) interpreted the Rubric in this sense,[25] as did the eighteenth century authorities.

But the very definite wording of the Rubric is fatal to this interpretation.

1. In the first place it says nothing about the First Prayer Book; and its careful wording throughout makes it unlikely that it should say one thing when it meant another. This part of the Rubric was composed, not by Cosin, but in 1559; ten years only after the publication of the First Prayer Book. Elizabeth must have known the date of her brother's accession, and of the First Prayer Book. What so simple as to refer to it?[26]

2. That First Prayer Book was not in use during any part whatever of the second year of Edward vi., and therefore the Ornaments of that Book could not possibly have been the ornaments used by authority of Parliament in that year. The second year of Edward vi. was, beyond any doubt, from Jan. 28, 1548 to Jan. 27, 1549.[27] The First Prayer Book received the authority of Parliament in the last week of that year, Jan. 21, 1549;[28] but the Act itself fixes the day on which it is to come in use as the Whitsunday following, June 9, 1549, or if it might be had sooner, then three weeks after a copy had been procured. So that the First Prayer Book could not possibly have been anywhere in use until some weeks (at the very earliest) after the third year of Edward vi. had begun; as a matter of fact the earliest edition bears the date 'the viii daye of March, in the third yere of the reigne of our Sovereigne Lorde Kynge Edward the vi.'[29]

Furthermore, the First Prayer Book makes no attempt to fix the limit as to ornaments and vestments to be used. If the Rubric refers to this Book it could not take a more uncertain standard. At the end of the Book[30] occurs the dissertation, 'Of Ceremonies, why some be abolished and some retained'; immediately after this dissertation comes the following heading, 'Certain notes for the more plain explication and decent ministration of things contained in this book,' after which come the notes as to the use of the surplice and other vestments, as to kneeling, crossing, and other gestures, as to the omission of the Litany, and of the Creed, Gloria and Homily on certain occasions. Nothing could look less like limiting the use of the old ornaments than this form of expression, 'certain notes.' Indeed we know from abundant evidence that the old ornaments were largely used under the First Prayer Book.[31]

Thus, even if the Rubric could be shown to refer to the ornaments used under the book, it cannot be honestly limited to those ornaments that are *mentioned* in that book; for many that were used are not mentioned (as altar-lights), some even that were indispensable are not mentioned (as the linen altar cloth). And in these omissions it follows the missals of Sarum, Bangor, York, and Hereford.[32]

Nor, indeed, does this reference of the Rubric to the First Prayer Book give much help to those who oppose ceremonial. For, besides allowing such gestures as crossing and knocking upon the breast, the Book orders the albe with vestment or cope, and tunicles[33] for 'the Supper of the Lord and the Holy Communion, commonly called the Mass,' the rochet, cope or vestment and pastoral staff for the bishop,[34] the chrisom-cloth,[35] the corporas cloth,[36] and wafer-bread.[37] It implies the use of further ornaments in giving directions for unction,[38] reservation for the sick,[39] and the burial of and Mass for the dead.[40] It is not, therefore, surprising that Bonner used the book, and that Gardiner expressed his approval of it.[41]

But, as a matter of plain fact, the Ornaments Rubric does refer behind even the First Prayer Book to the 'second year' of Edward vi, before that book had come into use, before one single ornament could have been abrogated by that book.

What then had the 'authority of Parliament' done by the second year in the matter of ornaments? Late in the first year (1547) an Act had been passed ordering the restoration of the primitive rule of Communion in both kinds,[42] and on the 8th of March in the next year the Order of Communion was issued.[43] This Order referred only to the communicating of the people, and was to be inserted in the old Latin service 'without varying of any other rite or ceremony of the Mass.' So then, we know that the old service and ceremonies, with this addition, continued in use throughout the second year, and until after the third year had begun. The only modifications as to ornaments were those effected by the Injunctions[44] of the Privy Council, issued in 1547, which ordered the removal of all shrines, and everything connected with them, of those images which had been abused by offerings and other superstitious observances, and of those pictures which represented feigned miracles.

The ornaments, therefore, ordered by our Church, are those of 1548, unless their use has been taken away by a rubric of the Book of Common Prayer.

The Ornaments Rubric is part of an Act of Parliament as well as of the Prayer Book; it was passed not only by Convocation but also by

Parliament in 1661-2. It is therefore just as statutably binding on us as the Canons of 1603 (indeed in many points it supersedes those Canons), or the latest Act of Parliament; and, what is of far more serious importance, it is just as ecclesiastically binding upon us as the rubrics which order the use of Morning and Evening Prayer or the reading of the Bible.

The only excuse for disobeying it in part (for no one neglects *all* its provisions) is the long disuse into which so many of those provisions have fallen. This disuse exempts those who disobey the Rubric from any legal or episcopal penalties,[45] it also gives the clergy a perfectly valid excuse for restoring the legal ornaments slowly, nay, in some cases it makes slow progress an absolute duty for them; but it does not alter the fact that all disobedience to the Rubric is lawlessness, and is against the mind of the Church of England.

In this connection one more aspect of the Ornaments Rubric has to be considered. It has often been assumed that it had been since its first enactment obsolete, until it was revived by a party of ritualists in the present reign.

This is not true. The neglect of the Ornaments Rubric was very gradual, and at the worst times of Hanoverian sloth it was still obeyed in many particulars. For instance, it was the sole authority for the use of any distinctive dress by the clergy at the times of their ministration. There are no other directions in our Prayer Book, and those of the Canons[46] were superseded by the re-enactment of the Rubric in 1662 with its special clause as to vestments. Again, certain ornaments which were constantly set up even in the reign of George III. are not elsewhere sanctioned in the Prayer Book; such are organs, stained glass, and pictures, all of which were strongly opposed by the Puritans. Again, the use of altar-candles was never entirely dropped in the English Church.[47]

I have shown in various places of this Handbook how gradual and unauthorised was the neglect of the Ornaments Rubric. A few more instances here may be useful, since want of knowledge on this subject is very widespread.

To take first the crucial case of incense. It may be a surprise to some to hear that incense was recommended by Herbert, used by Cosin and Andrewes, and many other seventeenth century divines, and also in the royal chapel at least in the reigns of Elizabeth and Charles I.; that a form for the consecration of censers was used by Andrewes,

Laud, and Sancroft, which brings the use down to 1685; and that when our modern ritualists revived it there were men living who might have seen it burnt in Ely Cathedral.[48]

The use of vestments was still more authoritative and widespread. To begin with the time of Elizabeth. Here is an inventory of the Church of St. Bartholomew, Smithfield, in 1574, fifteen years after the Ornaments Rubric had been issued:—

'Certayne things appertaining to ye Churche as followthe:—
Imprimis a communion cloth of redd silke and goulde.
Itm a communion coppe [cup] of silver withe a cover.
Itm a beriall cloth of redd velvet and a pulpitte clothe of ye same.
Itm two greene velvet quishins [cushions].
Itm a blewe velvet cope.
Itm a blewe silke cope.
Itm a white lynnen abe [albe] and a hedd cloth [amice] to the same.
Itm a vestment of tawney velvet. Itm a vestment of redd rought velvet.
Itm a vestment of greene silke with a crosse garde of redd velvet.
Itm a crosse bannor of redd tafata gilded.
Itm two stoles of redd velvet.
Itm two white surplices.
Itm two comunion table clothers.
Itm two comunion towels.'

The Canons of 1603, which were issued before the ritualistic revival of the Laudian prelates, and at a time when those in authority were hard put to it to enforce the minimum of decency, show us what was the minimum that was then thought tolerable. Canon 58 orders the surplice, hood, and tippet for parish churches. Canon 24 orders the cope for the celebrant, and the proper vestments for the gospeller and epistler in cathedrals.[49]

It is hardly necessary to repeat here that the cope was so used not only in cathedrals, but in some parish churches also in Charles I.'s reign. This vestment, which is now considered too ritualistic even in some churches where the eucharistic vestments are worn, was in constant use at Durham till nearly a century ago,[50] and has been retained till to-day at Westminster to do honour to the earthly king on state occasions. Indeed the Ornaments Rubric was frankly recognised in the eighteenth century, down to our own time, as 'still in force at this day.'[51] It was left to certain forensic casuists of the nineteenth to declare that it was not.

It is clear, then, if history, logic, and the English language have any meaning at all, that the duty of all loyal sons of the Church of England is to use the old ornaments.

How should they be used?

1. With tolerance. Because those who inserted the Rubric left its practice to the growth of voluntary obedience; because those who now disobey it can claim the protection of long prescription; and because, with the rapid decay of unreasoning prejudice, the general human instinct for ceremonial worship is reasserting itself among all parties with quite sufficient celerity.

2. With moderation. Because the old order to which we are referred was as a matter of fact very moderate, and singularly different in its real beauty to the fussy excess of Roman Catholic churches, and of those English churches which try (with indifferent success) to copy them. The rich ornaments of a great cathedral like St. Paul's or Salisbury were much modified in a small parish church; indeed one of the Sarum rubrics actually provides for those churches which had not even a proper font.[52] The full complement of ornaments is not to be expected of a small parish church; and the medieval altar was as simple as that of the more decent parish churches in the time of Queen Anne. On the other hand it must be remembered that even small churches, simple though they were, had many remarkably rich and beautiful ornaments.[53] This combination of richness with simplicity was a note of medieval times, when vulgarity as we have it was unknown, and the simplest domestic utensils were beautiful and refined. Vulgarity is due to a want of the sense of proportion.

3. With loyal exactness, so far as it is possible. Not on the principles of private judgment, which are so prevalent to-day, though they are condemned in this very connection by the 34th Article,[54] by the preface On Ceremonies,[55] and indeed by every Catholic authority. The 'publick and common order' belongs of right to the whole body of the faithful, and if it is tampered with by individual fancies must, in the nature of things, be gradually and inevitably degraded.

Not, either, by referring to the court of Rome, which has no authority in this country, and can only be followed here by a violent exercise of that private judgment which is essentially Protestant, under whatever name it may mask itself; which indeed cannot be copied with any remote approach to correctness while any part of our Prayer Book is used. Our Church has declared again and again her right to order her own ceremonies; and in this she has all Catholic precedent on her side. She has furthermore declared her intensely strong adherence to antiquity; and therefore distinctively Roman practices, which are almost entirely of seventeenth, eighteenth, or nineteenth century growth, are doubly opposed to the standard which she sets up. Our solemn vows make any rejection of our own traditional practices in favour of those from abroad utterly impossible for us.

Not, even, by the following of medieval Salisbury; for in many respects the rules of this particular cathedral were altered by the generations that came between their enactment and the second year of Edward vi., and also by the rubrics of our Prayer Book, which book expressly declares that as regards saying and singing (upon which depends a good deal of our ceremonial) there should be not the use of Sarum, or of any other diocese, but our national English use. This does not lessen the immense value of the Sarum books in interpreting our own rubrics; but it must never be forgotten that all the ceremonies of a magnificent cathedral cannot be applicable to a parish church; and, indeed, we know that they were never so applied. A great deal of harm has been done by the thoughtless use of the word 'Sarum,' when the statements of the Prayer Book should have led us to the only exact word 'English.' This has been especially the case in the matter of colours, which are dealt with in a section of this Handbook. It is not to the Rome or Paris of the nineteenth century, nor is it to the Salisbury of the fourteenth, that the Ornaments Rubric refers us, but to the England of 1548. And, if we break the Rubric in favour of Rome, we must not be surprised if others break it in favour of Geneva.

4. The ornaments must be used within the Prayer Book. There are a few who interpret this to mean that, where there are no services in the Prayer Book for certain ornaments the old services should be revived. But most hold that the rubric only 'directs that the ornaments required for the due execution of the rites contained in the Book of Common Prayer shall be those which were used for the like purpose at the date assigned.'[56] Without attempting to pronounce upon the subject, which would be beyond our province, it is clear that for the practical ends of such a Handbook as this the latter view is the more convenient to follow. Yet there cannot but be some exceptions to this rule; for the growing and irresistible need for

additional services has caused some of the old offices to be revived, and that with due permission. Which permission has been wisely given, lest worse things should befall, and is my excuse for suggesting in certain cases, with all due deference, the traditional method of carrying them out. It must also be remembered, though with caution, that the continuous use of the *Gloria Tibi* before the Gospel is a witness that an old form of words is not necessarily unlawful because it has been omitted from the Prayer Book.

5. Lastly, the ornaments must be used in the traditional way. The Prayer Book is generally regarded with a strong Hanoverian bias; and those ceremonies are looked upon as natural which have come to us from the worst period of lawlessness, sloth, and worldliness. Consequently, those who really try to get at the mind of the English Church are popularly regarded as lawless.

But a moment's thought will make it clear that the Prayer Book really requires of us a bias in exactly the opposite direction. We are to interpret it, not from the point of view of an Elizabethan Calvinist, or of a Georgian pluralist, or even of a Caroline ritualist, or of any 'private man,' but from that of Scripture, Tradition, and the Fathers. Nay, the command of the book is unmistakable: we are to interpret it in the spirit of a parson of the year 1548, who was conversant with the old ceremonial.

There is a wise saying of Thomas a Kempis, which, had it been remembered, would have averted many a disastrous misunderstanding of Holy Scripture,— that the Bible must be read in the same spirit in which it was written. May we not say that the same canon of interpretation, applied to the Prayer Book, would have averted both the former falling away and the latter chaos of ill-directed revival? The Prayer Book was written partly by primitive and medieval Christians, partly by those who translated and compiled it, skilled ritualists like Cranmer in one age and Cosin in another, who used many of the old ornaments,[57] and had a profound reverence for Catholic tradition. And, lest there should be any mistake, its users are all referred to the year when almost all the old ornaments were in daily, lawful, and universal use.

Just as the ornaments were for years after the compiling of our Liturgy used in the traditional way and with the usual ceremonies, so must we, subject to any later rubrics, use them. It would be clearly absurd, for instance, and against the mind of the Church, to put the verger into a chasuble, or to place a processional cross in the hands of the celebrant; it would be only a shade less absurd for a server to hold a banner unaccompanied by any procession; and, I venture to say, it would be almost as indefensible to use the censer in any novel or unauthorised manner. Our 34th Article is clear that no individual, however highly placed, may change the traditions or ceremonies of the Church. Any such attempt on the part of a bishop would lead to lamentable reprisals on that of his clergy; and, indeed, has so led during the past fifty years. The only possible principle of interpretation is that no ceremony is abolished for which the ornament is directed to be used, unless there is authority of the Church for abolishing it.

Indeed the Prayer Book does not pretend to be a complete ritual directory. That idea is a Romish one, and has only been attempted in the Church of Rome in modern times. Like the medieval missals, our Book is meagre in its ceremonial directions, leaving much to 'ancient custom,'[58] as Cosin himself said at the last Revision. It can be proved both in the Prayer Book and in the Sarum Missal that certain things have to be done for which there is no direction given.[59] Furthermore, the Prayer Book is a *paroissien* rather than a directory; and there were good reasons why its ceremonial should be quietly-left to tradition, as it was; for a too complete array of rubrics would have led to schism, and schism was more dreaded than disobedience in those days. Before 1662, the Puritans, as we have seen, were non-conformists in the strict and only correct meaning of that word, in the meaning which they themselves gave to it. Since then, non-conformity was still allowed among those Englishmen who remained in communion with the Church; the proper way of interpreting the rubrics was not followed, because for the sake of peace and comprehension the neglect of the 'interpretation rubric' was allowed. Thus it was that non-conformity became a tradition in the Church; and, curiously enough, those very churchmen who are popularly considered to be specially Anglican and law-abiding are to-day non-conformists in exactly the same sense as were the Puritans of the Elizabethan and Jacobean era.

This comprehensive tolerance of non-conformity to the Church's rubrics was wise and just. The history, indeed, of the eighteenth century shows that it was carried too far; the history of the seventeenth century shows that it was not able to avert the schism which it was designed to prevent. But it saved the Church from being swamped by Puritanism in those hard times, it kept the bulk of the nation in communion with the Catholic Church; and the history of our own century shows that this non-conformity was bound gradually to disappear as soon as the old prejudices began to die a natural death. This curious lax administration, through three centuries, of perfectly definite laws is a monument of our national indifference to logic; but it is also a monument of that profound and practical common-sense which is the peculiar characteristic of our race.

There can be no doubt that the only satisfactory settlement of the questions of ceremonial will be through the constitution of an authoritative committee of experts, such as is recommended by the present Archbishop of York. Such a committee, deciding all the questions brought before it with strict impartiality and with exact knowledge, will secure the support of all loyal churchmen, and will gradually establish throughout the land a type of service such as the Prayer Book contemplates, a service unequalled in Christendom for dignity, beauty, and reverence.

But meanwhile something must be done, both to satisfy the consciences of those who cannot be content with mere non-conformity, and to establish the ceremonial of the future on a sound foundation. No individual, or unauthorised committee of individuals, has any right to dictate in such a matter. But yet much may be done in the way of suggestion; for in the great majority of cases it is now certain on what lines a committee of experts would decide. Some things that are now common will no doubt have to be altered; but, as these grew up during the infancy of liturgical science in this country, and are due either to ignorance or to a rather wanton exercise of private judgment, it is far better that they should be altered at once. I can only say that in this Handbook I have tried to follow the most reliable acknowledged authorities, and to avoid giving my own private opinion (except in small practical matters not dependent upon ceremonial). I have tried to make it clear when it seemed necessary to give my own opinion. I have tried to be entirely faithful to the principles that are stated in the Introduction to this book.

But in matters of art I have dogmatised, because it is impossible to do otherwise. I have given my own opinions for what they are worth; but I think I can without peril say that such are the opinions also of the great body of artistic experts in this country. This book being practical, I make no apology for freely recommending those shops which in my opinion are the best for the parson to go to for certain things; for experience has taught me that without some guide of this kind it is impossible for any of us to furnish our churches aright.

Every one who writes about ceremonial is certain to be subject to one of two forms of criticism; either that his directions are too minute, or that they are not minute enough.

The answer to the first objection is plain in a practical book of this kind. No one is bound to follow them: it is safer, therefore, to give too many directions than too few. Half an hour with a blue pencil will reduce the ceremonial to the required simplicity; but faults of omission would take much longer to rectify.

Furthermore, there is undoubtedly a right and a wrong way of doing everything, and therefore it is just as well to do things in the right way; for unless one has an unusually large share of instinctive grace and tact, one will otherwise be in danger of making oneself, and also the service one is conducting (which is more important), appear uncouth, or queer, or ridiculous.

Ceremonial directions often appear at first sight to be over-minute. But all the manners of our everyday life are governed by rules quite as elaborate; only, being instructed in them from our earliest childhood, we do not notice them. Let any one write out a paper of directions for the conduct of a South Sea Islander at a London dinner-party, and he will find that the most meticulous ceremonies ever held in a church are far out-distanced. And yet a person who simplifies the ceremonial of the dinner-table over much becomes obviously disgusting in his behaviour.

The ancient traditions are not extravagant: they are really restraints upon private extravagance. They are, like those of society, the result of the accumulated experience of many centuries; and they were chosen because they were found to make the service run without hitch or possibility of accident, and to give a measure of grace and dignity even to those who are naturally awkward. How much of the old Catholic ceremonial has been retained, even among those who are most opposed to ceremonies, will be clear to any one who compares the worship of the barest church with that of a place of worship which has no such traditions, say of a mosque or a Chinese temple.

One has not to go far to notice how many of the clergy and other Church officials do as a matter of fact stand in very great need of a few elementary lessons in deportment. Such lessons are needed in all civilised society, not to make one stiff or ceremonious, but to prevent one being stiff, to make one natural and unaffected. Indeed the doings of some of the 'ritualistic' clergy that cause offence are really their own private ideas of what is reverent and seemly, and not those of Church tradition, which is essentially moderate and subdued. On the other hand, what would be thought of a state function, if those who took part in it behaved like an average cathedral choir? Yet one might expect as much trouble to be given to the service of the Church as to that of the State.

To those at the opposite extreme, who may urge that my suggestions are not minute enough, I would reply that my object has simply been to carry through the services of our Church, as they stand, with the ornaments that are ordered; and that, therefore, such ceremonies, for instance, as were used in some parts of the old Canon of the Mass are outside my province.

It is clear from the tenor of the Prayer Book that a simplification of ceremonial was intended; and therefore it is not necessary in a book of this sort to work in every old ceremony whether there is a place for it or not. Furthermore, it must be remembered that much of the ceremonial that we see is not taken from our own traditions, but from foreign sources. If even the old 'ceremonies' are convicted by our Prayer Book of 'great excess and multitude,' much more must those of later continental ritualists be out of the question for us. The mind of the Prayer Book indubitably is to simplify rites and ceremonies without detracting either from their grace, significance, or richness. The Prayer Book wisely considers that our people have not the same way of expressing themselves as the Southern races; and so, while we 'condemn no other nations,' we have no right to impose upon ourselves or upon others that bondage to fresh *minutiae* of ceremonial which other races, rightly or wrongly, consider needful.

At the same time, it may be urged against me that I have omitted one or two matters for which there is much to be said. My reply is that I do so, as the lawyers say, without prejudice, and simply on the ground that, as they are hardly used at all, their treatment at the present time would but encumber a volume that is only a handbook for the parson of an ordinary parish, and pretends to be merely practical.

With regard to the whole of the foregoing argument, it must be remembered that, were it possible to disprove every point of it, nearly all the ornaments of the Rubric (including the censer, the two lights— or one at the least,—the chasuble, dalmatic, cope, etc.) would still be statutably binding upon us.[60] For they are ordered by the unrepealed parts of the ancient canon law. The seventh clause of 25 Hen. VIII. 'continues in its former force the whole of the canon law which is not repugnant to the laws, statutes, and customs of the realm, nor to the damage and hurt of the royal prerogative.'

It seems certain that the present increase in beauty of worship, which is noticeable among ail parties in the English Church, and indeed outside it as well, will continue to grow, till Mohammedanism is left as the only religion that discards the almost universal human instinct for richness of ceremonial worship. Yet it appears to be not less certain that freedom will be a mark also of the future, rather than strict ceremonial uniformity. We need not regret this tendency; for such uniformity never did obtain in the time when the Church was at peace. Its attempted enforcement, in Rome or elsewhere, is a sign that the Church Catholic is divided.

This book must not, therefore, be taken as the attempt of an unauthorised person to dictate to his brethren. Whether they conform little or much is a matter for themselves to decide. I have only tried to show what it is that our Church requires. Those requirements leave many degrees of ceremonial open to us, even within the limits of strict conformity; and the tolerance of non-conformity in the Church allows in practice an even greater freedom. But, whether the ceremonial used is little or much, the services of our Church should at least be conducted on the legitimate lines, if only that they may be freed from what is anomalous, irreverent, tawdry, or grotesque.

Notes

1 Bishop of Rochester's Address to his Diocesan Conference in October 1898.

2 'Although the Law given from God by Moses, as touching ceremonies and rites, do not bind Christian men.' —7th Article.

3 Ex. xxx. 34.

4 Mal. i. 11.

5 S. Luke i. 9, and also 11.

6 S. Matt. ii. 11.

7 Rev. v. 8, R.V.

8 Rev, viii. 3, 4, A.V. and R.V.

9 It should be noticed that the first words of this Preface are generally misunderstood. 'The phrase,' says Bishop Barry, 'ascribing to the Church of England "the middle way between two extremes" has become celebrated, being supposed to be a description of her general principle and policy. A glance at the context will, however, show that it refers simply to the policy adopted in the revisions of the Prayer Book,' that is, between too much stiffness in refusing or too much readiness in admitting variations. *Teacher's Prayer Book (in loc.)*.

10 'We do the Anglican reformers a certain 'injustice,' says Canon Daniel, commenting on this Preface, 'in designating them by the negative name of Protestants. . . . The best name is that which they themselves rejoiced in—the name of Catholics.' (Daniel *on the P. B.* 26.

11 The reference here is to out-door apparel.

12 *First P. B.* 71.

13 *Ibid.*

14 This is made still clearer by the 30th Canon touching the very same point of the abuse of ceremonies. 'But the abuse of a thing doth not take away the lawful use of it. Nay, so far was it from the purpose of the Church of England to forsake and reject the Churches of Italy, France, Spain, Germany, or any such like Churches, in all things which they held and practised, that, as the Apology of the Church of England confesseth, it doth with reverence retain those ceremonies, which doth neither endamage the Church of God, nor offend the minds of sober men; and only departed from them in those particular points, wherein they were fallen both from themselves in their ancient integrity, and from the Apostolical Churches, which were their first founders.' Here the intense conservative reverence of the English Church for the old ceremonies, and its desire to destroy nothing that could be defended on the ground of antiquity, is made even clearer. But it must be confessed

that those who try to read in the broad tolerance of this Canon a sanction for the imitation of modern Roman Catholic customs, are hard pressed for an excuse.

15 And so indeed they were: *e.g.* an entry in the register in Darsham Church—'A license granted to Mr. Thomas Southwell to eat meat in Lent, aged 82, and sickly, by John Eachard [Vicar], for which he paid 6s. 8d. for the use of the poor in Darsham, according to the statute, March 4, 1638.'

16 James ii. 2, 3.

17 See *e.g.* Cartwright's *Second Admonition to Parliament*.

18 The bishop's rochet is the only vestment mentioned in our Prayer Book; and it is merely a part of his out-door dress.

19 See introduction.

20 That this Prayer Book was not regarded as abolishing the old religion is shown by the fact that, of 9400 Marian clergy, only about 200 refused to take the oath of supremacy and accept the new Prayer Book. Elizabeth indignantly refused to send a representative to the Council of Trent because England was summoned as a Protestant, and not as a Catholic, country. She said, in her letter to the Roman Catholic princes, 'that there was no new faith propagated in England; no new religion set up but that which was commanded by our Saviour, practised by the primitive Church, and approved by the Fathers of the best antiquity.'

Of Elizabeth's first and favourite Archbishop, Parker, so dispassionate a historian as Mr. Gardiner says:—' He fully grasped the principle that the Church of England was to test its doctrines and practices by those of the Church of the first six hundred years of Christianity, and he, therefore, claimed for it catholicity, which he denied to the Church of Rome; whilst he had all Cranmer's feeling for the maintenance of external rites which did not directly imply the existence of beliefs repudiated by the Church of England.'—*Students History*, 430.

21 Cardwell, *Hist. of Conferences*, 314

22 *Ibid.* 351.

23 Not copes and surplices only, but altars, frontals, cloths, cushions and hangings, fonts, organs, candlesticks, basons, crosses and altar-

plate had been abolished by the House of Commons, 1640-3 (Perry, *Purchas J.*, 228-9).

24 These words are not necessarily Erastian; they merely safeguard the rubric from any doubts that could arise through the unconstitutional action of individuals, which was so rife in the time of Edward.

25 But Cosin's well-known Notes on the Ornaments Rubric (vol. v. 232, 438) make it clear that he understood the Rubric as covering all the ornaments *that were used under* the First Prayer Book, and much more than were mentioned in it:—'*As were in use, etc.* Among other ornaments of the Church that were then in use, the setting of two lights upon the communion-table or altar was one, appointed by the King's *Injunctions* (set forth about that time [1547, the *first* year], and mentioned or ratified by the Act of Parliament here named) ... that two lights only should be placed upon the altar to signify the joy and splendour we receive from the light of Christ's blessed Gospel. *Bene B. Lutherus in formula missae sive Communionis, quam Witten-burgensi Ecclesiae anno superioris seculi vicesimo tertio praescripsit, Nee candelas (inquit) nec thurificationem prohibimus, sed nec exigimus; esto hoc liberum.*

'The particulars of these ornaments ... are referred not to the fifth year of Ed. vi ... for in that fifth year were all ornaments taken away (but a surplice only) ... but to the second year of that king when his Service-book and *Injunctions* were in force by authority of parliament. And in those books many other ornaments are appointed; as, two lights to be set upon the altar or communion-table, a cope or vestment for the priest ... and those ornaments of the Church, which *by former laws*, not then abrogated, were in use, *by virtue of the statute 25 Henry VIII.* [1533-4], and for them the provincial constitutions are to be consulted, such as have not been repealed.'

Thus Cosin refers the Rubric, not to the First Book only, but also to the statute of 1533, and to the Injunctions of the first year of Edward vi., 1547. Even the latter expressly forbade 'the varying of any other rite or ceremony in the Mass (until other order shall be provided),' which order was provided by the First Prayer Book, published in 1549. That Prayer Book, however, abolished very little. The mistake that people make in this connection is to confuse the ornaments *mentioned by* the First Book with those *in use under* the First Book; it is clearly the latter that Cosin means.

26 Indeed Archbishop Sandys (then Bishop of Winchester) wrote at the time, 'The Parliament draweth towards an end; the last Book of Service is gone through with a Proviso to retain the Ornaments which were used in the *First and Second* years of Ed. vi.' Sandys himself disliked the ornaments and continued, 'One gloss upon the text is that we shall not be *forced* to use them.' It did not occur to him to gloss the text by a reference to the First Prayer Book.

27 See *e.g.* the table of the regnal years in the *Dictionary of English History*, 651. Edward came to the throne Jan. 28, 1547.

28 It could not have received the royal assent till March 14, 1549.

29 The various imprints are:—*Mense Martii* (4), *Mense Maii, Mense Junii,* and *Mense Julii,* all 1549.

30 Chapter VI.

31 *E.g.* the inventory of Beckenham Parish Church in the *sixth* year of Edward vi. describes (in addition to two copes, nine vestments, two vestments for deaon and sub-deacon, and patens, two chalices, four corporax clothes, four steeple bells, the Bible and Paraphrases of Erasmus) the following ornaments not mentioned in the First Book, – one pax, one crosse, one pix, two sacring bells, sixteen alter-clothes, six towels, two hand towels, six corporax cases, three little pillows standing on the altar, a case clothe of red solke, two blake palls, eight olde banner clothes for the crosse, two sepulchre clothes, and other hangings (*Record Office,* Q. R. *Church Goods* 3/43).

32 The evidence for lights is elsewhere.

33 *First Prayer Book,* 65-6.

34 *Ibid.* 171.

35 *Ibid.* 106, 159.

36 *Ibid.* 75.

37 *Ibid.* 90.

38 *Ibid.* 106, 140.

39 *Ibid.* 142, 144.

40 *Ibid.* 146-157.

41 *Gasquet, Ed. VI, and B.C.P.* 281-5.

42 1st Edw. vi. cap. 1.

43 It was approved by Convocation of the Province of Canterbury, and was held to receive parliamentary authority from 31 Hen. VIII. cap. 8, which gave the authority of Parliament, under certain restrictions, to royal Proclamations.

44 Their parliamentary authority is disputable, its only basis being the unconstitutional Act of Hen. VIII. above referred to. See Perry, *Lawful Church Ornaments,* 26, 28; Collier, ii. 213-225.

45 But—'By the Law of England no statute can fall into desuetude ... if once a Court is called upon to carry it into execution, it must do so.' —Lushington, *Liddell Judgement,* 35.

46 *E.g.* Archdeacon Sharp in 1746,—'Upon the 58 Canon ... I need say the less because it is superseded by the Rubric before the Common Prayer, in 1661, which is statute-law.' (Quoted in Perry, *Purchas J.,* 114.)

47 Cf. *Lincoln Judgement, in loc.*

48 'It was the constant practice at Ely to burn incense at the altar in the Cathedral, till Dr. Thos. Green, one of the Prebendaries, and now (1779) Dean of Salisbury, a finical man, who is always taking snuff up his nose, objected to it, under the pretence that it made his head to ache.' Cf. Walcott, *Customs of Cathedrals,* 160.

49 It was a few years after this date, when Andrewes was Bishop of Ely (1605-9), that he used in his chapel 'two candlesticks with tapers, the daily furniture for the altar, a cushion for the service-book, silver and gilt canisters for the wafers,' and also among other things 'a little boate out of which the frankincense is poured, a tricanale for the water of mixture.' —Prynne, *Canterburie's Doome.*

50 Warburton threw his off in a pet, because it disturbed his wig, and the use of copes at Durham 'does not seem to have been totally discontinued until 1784.' —*Abbey and Overton,* ii. 467.

51 Nicholls in his preface to Cosin's annotated Prayer Book (1710). Also Bishop Gibson, the author of the *Codex Juris Ecclesiastici* (1711). Perry (*Purchas J.*) gives a catena of legal and ecclesiastical authorities who admitted this fact, down to 1845.

52 In this falling below our own 81st Canon. the rubric orders the parish priest to have a *'fontem, lapideum, integrum et honestum.'* if he can; but if not, *'habeat vas conveniens ad baptismum quod aliis usibus nullatanus deputetur, nec extra ecclesiam deportetur.'*

53 See Dr. Jessop's two most valuable articles on England before the Great Pillage, in the *Nineteenth Century* for 1897.

54 'Whosoever through his private judgment, willingly and purposely, doth openly break the traditions and ceremonies of the Church,' etc.

55 'The appointment of which order pertaineth not to private men; therefore no man ought to take in hand, nor presume to appoint or alter any publick or common order in Christ's Church,' etc.

56 See the influentially signed 'Knightsbridge Memorandum' of May 2nd, 1898.

57 This is not altered by the fact that Cranmer changed his views more than once. In 1536 he could say:—'As vestments in God's service; sprinkling holy water; giving holy bread; bearing candles on Candlemas Day; giving of ashes on Ash Wednesday; bearing of palms on Palm Sunday; creeping to the Cross, and kissing it, and offering unto Christ before the same on Good Friday; setting up the sepulchre of Christ; hallowing of the font, and other like exorcisms and benedictions, and laudable customs: that these are not to be contemned and cast away, but continued to put us in remembrance of spiritual things.' But in Edward vi.'s time, he tried to put a stop to the use of ashes, palms, and the Candlemas lights, in 1547, though the 'holy bread' and sprinkling with holy water are still enjoined in 1548 (Strype i. 62; Cardwell, 38, 56).

58 See an interesting passage in Mr. Wakeman's *History of the Church of England* (280):—'If the New Zealander, made famous by Macaulay, should chance to find a copy of the present Prayer Book while he is visiting the ruins of St. Paul's ... he would be sorely puzzled to extract from the rubrics anything like a complete order of service.' Of the First Book he says:—'The fact is, the book is unintelligible except on the theory that it presupposed the existence of a well-known system, and only gave such directions as were necessary to carry out and explain the changes which had been made.' Some directions that had been in the First Book were omitted simply in order to make the rubrics as terse as possible, the revisers evidently relying upon

custom: *e.g.* the omission of 'or Deacon' in the rubric for the reading of the Gospel.

59 The priest for instance must return the child after he has baptized it, and it is a difficult question whether this should be before or after the signing with the cross. The Sarum Missal provides the priest with neither surplice nor albe.

60 Blunt and Phillimore, *Book of Church Law*, p. 23. The whole matter is dealt with in chap. ii. of that book. See also a recent article in the *Law Times*, quoted by Dean Luckock, *The Ritual Crisis*, p. 54.

CHAPTER I
THE CHOIR, NAVE, AND THEIR FURNITURE

Little need be said about the Choir, as so much must depend upon the architecture of the church. It should not be crowded with benches and desks, which has a very bad effect, but kept as open as possible. Where there is little room, it is far better not to have a surpliced choir; so that only stalls for the clergy and a few seats for the servers will be needed.

The stalls for the clergy will vary according to the size and customs of the church. In large churches as well as in collegiate churches returned stalls were formerly used.[1] The clergy will need an extra shelf for books; and a similar shelf for the men, partitioned between each seat, will be useful. It is my experience that the boys behave better if they have nothing at all to kneel up against. They will then kneel bolt upright, with nothing to screen them, on a strip of matting (say of dark green or red); and this will also give the choir a more open look.

No wood or metal work that can possibly come in the way should have sharp edges or corners. And no nails should be allowed to be fixed in the wood by those who carry out decorations.

The lighting of choirs by flaring gas-standards is a practice much to be avoided (still more so when two gaudy brass standards are placed near the altar). These things are nearly always very offensive in appearance: they get in the way: they are costly: they waste a great deal of gas; and they contribute towards spoiling and dirtying everything in the church. There are many other ways of managing the light. For instance incandescent burners may be fixed out of sight at the side of the choir; in which case their reflectors should throw the light on to the stalls; and two burners on each side will suffice for a not very large church. If the burners are fixed on standards it is best that these should be plain and stand in the midst of the benches: a shade to throw the light on the books will be useful to the singers, will try the eyes of the congregation less, give a better effect in the chancel, and economise gas. If oil-lamps are used, they too should be well shaded. In those churches that are fortunate enough to have electric light, it is generally better not to use the old gas-fittings (which may conveniently be got rid of at the installation); for electric lighting lends itself to peculiarly light and graceful methods. Anything like throwing a theatrical light on to the altar is strongly to be condemned. Gas or electric lights on the altar itself are intolerable. The general rules about all lighting, whether in nave or choir, should be,—that it be of as simple and unobtrusive nature as possible, that, if possible, it be not obtained by naked gas-jets burning to waste, that it be not placed at any height, but that the principal aim be to place it near to where it is wanted for the people to see their books, so that there is as much quiet shade in the church as possible. The less gas is burned the better. People are more drawn to and impressed by a church that is not filled with flaring light, though often they do not know the reason; and the present craving for a fussy crowd of candles on the altar is in great measure caused by the want of a reasonable proportion of light and shade in the rest of the church.

The service books should be well bound and stamped on the outside 'Choir' with a number, 'Choir Boys' with a number, and 'Clergy Decani,' or 'Cantoris,' etc. The boys should not be allowed to use any but those marked for them, as they have incurable destructive tendencies.

Hymn-papers should be filled in every week by the librarian, and placed one in each clergy stall, and two or three on each shelf for the choir. If they are printed altogether in red ink, the numbers will be more easily seen. It will also lessen the danger of false numbers being given out, if the place for the hymns be arranged in a column distinct from that for the chants, etc.

If the public notices that are to be read are written in a book, it serves to keep a useful record.

The Rood-Loft.—There can be little doubt that the most appropriate position theologically, as well as the most impressive, for the Rood or Crucifix is the ancient place on the chancel-screen, or, when there is no screen, on a beam running across the chancel arch. Reverence would suggest a great reserve in the use of crucifixes, which should not be dotted about the church in the way one sometimes sees. Nothing can well be more impressive than the use of one large crucifix on the screen or beam, and that alone. Figures of St. Mary and St. John were generally placed on either side of the Rood, and sometimes other figures also. The Rood-loft was a common place also for the organ and for musicians. Two, four, or six candles on the Rood-loft are in conformity with ancient custom,[2] and look most impressive if the church is kept in proper shade: they also have a good effect in daylight.

There are many good ways of disposing the organ. To block up a chapel with it is a bad way. The recent committee under the Bishop of Chester, which reported on the subject, showed that, for the sake of the instrument itself, it should not be crammed into positions of this sort. Our old country churches were not built to contain a large organ; there is no place for one, and therefore a chapel, often the only chapel, has been taken, to the destruction of the church's beauty and the great detriment of the organ's power. If the little Positive Organ, charming in appearance and excellent in tone, had been invented earlier, many a lovely old church would have been spared from hideous defacement. In larger churches some kind of organ-loft should be built. Organ-pipes should be left their natural colour.

There can be little doubt that the best arrangement both for music and for ceremonial in most churches is the old one of a west gallery, containing both organ and choir. This has the additional advantage of allowing for a mixed choir. The choristers can still take part in the procession, slipping off their surplices in the vestry, or going as they are into the gallery, when the procession is over. There is nothing particularly Catholic about a surpliced choir.

The Pulpit may be in almost any part of the church, the usual place being at the side of the nave. My own opinion is that the south side is the best for every one who is not left-handed; for the preacher, having his stronger side towards the people, is able to speak right across the church with more ease and self-command.

It is curious to notice how few pulpits are well placed or adequately fitted. As a rule they are pushed too far back against the chancel, and too much at the side of the church. Often they are half under a pier-arch, and the preacher as a consequence has to strain his voice in order to be heard, or is not heard by half the congregation. The old architects seldom made this mistake; they placed their pulpits well into the nave, and the preacher stood high enough to have a good command of his hearers.

Generally, too, of late years, expensive and very ugly stone pulpits have been set up. Of course, there is nothing wrong in itself about a stone pulpit; but a wooden one has these great advantages—that it is warm, smooth, and clean to the preacher's hand; that it *furnishes* a church, giving it warmth and colour; and that it can be easily moved.

If an immovable stone pulpit is to be set up, a small platform should first be knocked together, and carefully tried in different positions; it should be moved about until the spot is found, where (1) the voice rings truest and clearest with least effort, (2) gesture becomes most easy and unstrained, (3) the largest part of the congregation can be seen. It will generally be found that the same place will be best for all three purposes. In the case, for instance, of a church with two aisles; if the pulpit be brought well away from the pier-arches, it will be found not only that the acoustics are much improved, but also that he can see (and consequently be seen by) a far larger proportion of those who sit in the aisles. Or again, in a church with no aisles, if, instead of the pulpit being stuck against the wall, it project into the church, the preacher will not only find it easier to speak, but also to move, having no longer the fear of hitting the wall.

The pulpit should not, as a rule, be east of the easternmost row of seats, but should project a row or two into the seats on its side. As for height, I would suggest that the floor of the pulpit be not lower than the shoulders of the people when they are sitting down.

In the pulpit itself everything should be avoided that tends to make a preacher nervous or awkward. The steps to the pulpit are often better behind and out of sight, but in this case there should be a door, or at least a wooden bar, so that the occupant need not fear the fate of Eli. The sides of the pulpit should not be so low down that the hands dangle helplessly: Englishmen as a rule find their hands rather in the way, and they will speak much better, and avoid fingering their garments much more, if they can rest their hands quite comfortably on the sides of the pulpit. I would suggest 38 to 42 inches as a convenient height for men of average size; it is best to err on the side of height. Where the sides of the pulpit are too low, a rounded wooden rail can easily be fitted on to them, and it can very often be made to look well: the rail gives a rest for the fingers, it makes gesture more ready, the hands not having to be lifted so high, and at the same time it leaves the top of the pulpit (which should be at least 4 inches broad) quite free for books. Every pulpit should also have a shelf, sloping inwards, with a little ledge, large enough to hold the necessary books, and on the front side only. On the shelf there should be always a decent bible, a prayer book and hymn book, and a copy of the bidding prayer (which may be written on the fly-leaf of the prayer book). These books should not be too large to be put conveniently on the shelf, as anything that is in danger of tumbling-over adds to the constraint of the preacher. They should be stamped 'Pulpit,' and on no account ever be removed.

There should be always a desk for those who use notes or manuscript. This desk should not be made of cheap, shaky metal with thin edges. It should be substantial, with rounded edges that do not cut the hands. It should be firm, and readily adjustable both as to height and slope. Metal is better for this purpose than wood. But here as elsewhere it is well to remember that there is nothing particularly ecclesiastical or sacred about brass. It is better to cover it with a cloth, but the Church nowhere orders that such cloths should follow the colour of the seasons. The desk should look across to the opposite corner of the church, and not due west.

A round hole should be made on the shelf under the desk, to hold a watch, even if there is a clock in the church; for some men are short-sighted. The congregation will often have cause to be grateful if there is a clock within sight of the pulpit. In most small churches a plain round clock on the west gallery or wall will be best.

A small fixed seat may be set in a very large pulpit, but not in one of average size (36 inches inside diameter). Many old pulpits are only 30 inches across. Although tastes differ in the matter, it is often true that a large pulpit makes a fidgety preacher.

If there is a tumbler of water, it must be kept in an absolutely safe place; for instance, in a niche under the front shelf.

The question of sounding-boards depends upon the acoustic properties of the church. Often a curtain of tapestry behind the preacher will be an assistance: it also serves to rest the eyes of the congregation. A hanging round the front of the pulpit, covering the sides but not the base, may often hide a multitude of architectural sins.

In nothing are pulpits more badly managed than in the method of lighting. It may be laid down as an axiom that the lights should be turned down during the sermon; for this disposes the congregation to listen and not to stare about, rests their eyes, purifies the atmosphere, lessens the heat, spares the decorations, and reduces expense. Therefore the pulpit must have an independent supply of light of its own.

This should not be supplied by two unguarded candles on the shelf, unless the preacher is absolutely determined to court martyrdom. As a matter of fact, however, when preachers find themselves placed so near the fire, they take such care to avoid it that they remain throughout their discourse as impassive as statues. When the candles are guarded, the preacher is equally under restraint; for he is afraid of breaking the glass, and the fear of being ridiculous makes him awkward. No candle-bracket of any sort or kind on the shelf, or within possible reach of the preacher, is tolerable.

There remains another common alternative, that of placing a gas-bracket near the pulpit; but, if the pulpit projects sufficiently into the church, the gas-bracket will often be too far away. And in any case it will need a separate connection.

But it is still open to grave objection. If there is a gas-burner, candle, or other naked light near the pulpit, it will be very trying to the eyes of the congregation; it will thus cause them to look anywhere but at the preacher (whom indeed it often renders nearly invisible). Besides this, it generally gives a very poor light for the notes on the desk.

What is wanted is a flood of light on the desk, and a clear light on the preacher, with no visible flame at all. This can be easily obtained by hanging a lamp over the pulpit. The lamp should hang from a chain, fixed either to the roof, or, if the wall is not too far, to an iron bracket projecting from the wall some height above.

It should be suspended rather in front of the preacher and over the desk, at such a height that it can just be reached by any one in the pulpit, which will be found to mean that it is well out of the way of the most violent gesticulation. A pulley and chains will be convenient for tending the lamp. This lamp will of course be shaded. If a silk shade is used, it must be quite plain: red, or green, or dark yellow are good colours, lined with white. But the best plan of all is to have a copper reflector round the top of the chimney with a copper cup round the flame; in this way the rays of light are reflected with clear mellow brightness on to the desk and the preacher, while no flame at all is visible. The best designed lamps of this kind are made by Mr. W. A. S. Benson, 82 New Bond Street. They burn crystal oil, and can be lighted and turned out as easily as gas. Lamps need to be lacquered, as otherwise they are difficult to clean. It is best to light them before the service.

The Lectern may be beautiful or ugly, artistic or commercial, according to the spirit of the people who gave it. It can be cheap or dear, of wood or metal, according to their means; but it may be something other than a brass eagle without any offence against orthodoxy. One thing is essential to it,—that the desk be of a convenient height and angle, and do not come between the reader's head and the congregation. There is plenty of ancient precedent for much higher lecterns, but they were used for singing the service in the choir, and not for reading to the people. Like the pulpit, the lectern should be placed where the voice is best heard, for our rubric (as well as common sense) orders that the reader shall so stand as he may best be heard. It may be on the opposite side to the pulpit, and not too near the chancel. It should stand on a platform at least a foot above the floor of the nave. From the platform to the lower edge of the desk 48 inches is a good height.

Book-markers are a convenience, but not an ecclesiastical ornament, needing a particular treatment. To change them with the seasons is a piece of fancy ritual, which may be harmless, but is at any rate unnecessary, and rather damaging to the book. Red or blue are good colours. Reverence would suggest a sparing use in these and similar things of very sacred symbols.

Lectern-cloths are among the ornaments of our rubric, and often they will greatly improve the appearance of a lectern. The usual pattern is, however, not a good one: the lectern-cloth should be a strip of handsome material (not embroidered for preference) as wide as the desk, and long enough to hang not only over the front, but over the desk to a longer distance down the back. Cloths of this sort are better fringed at the ends, and sometimes also at the sides. There is no reason why they should follow the colour of the seasons, though they may be put away in Lent and either replaced by some older or more sombre cloths, or the lectern left bare. Of all things of this kind it is well to bear in mind that it is better to spend a fair sum on one of good material than to waste the same amount on four or five cheap ones. One bad result of this multitude of changeable material has been that the lesser feasts and fasts of the Church are often not marked at all. Only the frontal need be changed.

The Litany Desk or Faldstool is not proved to have been in use at the time of the rubric; but, as in the first year of Edward vi. it was ordered that in parish churches 'the priests, with other of the quire, shall kneel in the midst of the church, and sing or say the litany,' a desk may have come into use as a matter of convenience. Grindal in 1563 orders the Litany to be said 'in the midst of the people.' Cosin, in 1627, as Archdeacon of the East Riding enquires, 'Have you ... a little faldstool, or desk, with some decent carpet over it, in the middle aley of your church, whereat the Litany may be said?'[3] The position of the faldstool is discussed.

The desk, then, had at this time a 'carpet' *i.e.* a cloth on it, which, of course, like other cloths of this nature need not follow the colour of the season. If it stands in the middle alley of the nave, it should be at an ample distance from the chancel-steps, with plenty of room on either side of it, so as not to be in the way. If possible it should be a substantial roomy structure in wood. The tendency is to make them too high and too narrow in the shelf.

The Font should, according to Canon 81, be of stone, and 'set in the ancient usual place,' *i.e.* near the church door; this was again insisted on by the Bishops at the Savoy Conference;[4] the font was never in England placed in a special chapel or baptistry. As the rubric in our baptismal service orders the font to be filled afresh at each baptism, a drain is absolutely necessary. The Puritan practice of putting 'pots, pails, or basons' in it to hold the water was steadily condemned by our bishops from Parker downwards. The font should have a cover, which may be a simple lid or an architectural feature. Covers to fonts are constantly ordered from the time of St. Edmund of Canterbury to as late a date as that of Cosin. Care should be taken at festivals, if the font is decorated, to keep the top of it clear. When the font is ornamental in itself it is better not to decorate it.

Pews are by no means a Protestant invention, and in some ways they are better than chairs. They should, however, always be low, and the alleys both in aisles and nave should be much wider than usual. There are a good many old churches in England which show the medieval arrangement of low pews. They are like separate islands of low wood-work, two in the nave and one in each aisle, with plenty of open space at the west end. To leave thus wide alleys, and a clear bay at the west where the font stands, is a great help to the architecture of the church, and gives room for the proper management of processions. Movable chairs can always be added when necessary.

Pictures and Images are legal in the Church of England, at least so long as they do not commemorate 'feigned miracles,' and are not abused by superstitious observances, but are for a memorial only. Their destruction was the act of lawless violence, and their use has never been entirely discontinued.

The special series, called the Stations of the Cross, has, however, no authority; for these were never in use in England, being of comparatively modern date. And, as they are exclusively connected with a special service, they cannot be defended as if they were so many separate pictures. It may be added that, while in Roman Catholic churches they are generally kept in due proportion by the multitude of other pictures, of images, shrines, etc., in an English church they tend to give an undue prominence to one part of our Lord's life and work.

Photographs do not look well in a church, and even autotypes should be used very sparingly. Pictures with colour are wanted, and original paintings if possible. Some Arundels and some of the Fitzroy Picture Society's lithographs look extremely well. The Arundel Society has given over the remainder of its stock to the S.P.C.K., but nearly all the best are now out of print. The Fitzroy Pictures are kept at Messrs. Bell's, the Publishers, York Street, Covent Garden.

The choice of pictures lays a very solemn responsibility upon the parson; for many who see them will have their ideas of the Christian religion formed or modified by what they see. They may, for instance, form the impression that weak sentimentality, or theatrical self-consciousness, is the religion of Christendom. On the other hand they may learn to see in it sincerity, depth, and strength. Need I say that this is even more true of images?

The placing of pictures on the walls is a matter for the architect, and cannot safely be attempted by amateurs.

Shriving-pews were sometimes used in old times; but their shape is not known, and their use was not general. For many reasons it is better nowadays to hear confessions in the open church, either at a seat or pew by the wall, or in some accessible chapel.

Holy water stoups are ornaments of the rubric; and there seems to be no serious reason against their use. If not built into the masonry they were often made of metal or earthenware, and hung near the doors.[5]

One or more alms-boxes should be placed near the doors of the church, and clearly marked 'For the Poor,' 'For Church Expenses,' etc. These boxes are generally now of flimsy wood screwed on to the wall. As a result they offer great temptations to any thief with tools about him, and are used as an argument against open churches. It is a matter of common-sense that a box containing money in a public place (for the church is a public place) should be very strong. The old boxes that have come down to us are formidable looking things, heavily bound with iron. At the present day we can do even better.

Small iron alms-boxes of the 'safe' type are sold by any good church shop. They should be cemented into the wall.

Notice-boards should be kept very neatly, and this needs among other things that each corner of each notice should be pinned down with a drawing-pin. Where there are several boards, it is a good plan to keep one for notices of the week, another in a less conspicuous position for notices of a more permanent character, and another for receipts. A card for the names of the sick and departed, for whom the prayers of the congregation are desired, can hardly be dispensed with in a town parish. And at the present day it seems really necessary to post up in a prominent position the card 'Whosoever thou art' which is published by the S.P.C.K.

Hymn-boards are very useful, but sometimes there is not enough room on them when there are processionals or extra hymns. The day should be given at the top, so that every one can find the Psalms; and if a psalm is sung for the introit according to the First Prayer Book, it will save bother (and also the expense of introit books) if a piece of wood is provided with the word 'Introit' to hang over the word 'Day,' for the Holy Eucharist. The verger is generally the best person to look after the hymn-board.

Devotional books for private reading are an admirable institution in a church; they encourage people to make use of it, besides assisting meditation and helping to dissipate prejudice. The Bible and other books were formerly kept on a desk for folk to read; the custom of keeping books in church had come in as early as 1488, and in the seventeenth century devotional books were common in church. A small book-case may be hung near the west end, and supplied with a good selection of books, stamped with the name of the church.

Chapels are required by our Bishops, following the ancient practice, to be enclosed by some kind of open screen with doors. A chapel needs an altar with a foot-pace, and a credence, all of which may be smaller than those belonging to the chancel. Minor altars are not allowed unless they stand in a chapel. Chapels are intended for the Eucharist, not for choir offices.

Of all the objectionable ways of warming a church that of noisy iron gratings on the floor is one of the worst. They have a power of spoiling the effect of the architecture which is curiously beyond their importance; they are a danger at weddings and at other occasions; and they harbour rats.

No alterations or additions should be made in the architecture or furniture of a church until a faculty is obtained from the Bishop. The cost of a faculty for minor alterations (if unopposed) is £2, 2s.

There should always be benches in the Church Porch. An open wire door to let air into the church is useful in the summer, and the porch itself should have gates.

The verger should have a cupboard near the west end of the church, where his gown and wand and the alms-plates should be kept, and also magazines, additional hymn-books, and such like things. In new churches provision should be made in the wall for a cupboard of this sort.

The parish church belongs to the people, not only during service time, but all through the day. It is not the parson's private property: he is one of the trustees for it, and his duty is to keep it at the people's service. It is really inexcusable to exclude them from it at any time of the day. If all the doors are kept freely open it is safer than it would be with only one entrance; for a thief would have to keep a watch at all the entrances. As a matter of fact, thieves generally find it safer, for this reason, to break into a *locked* church. But the church is a public place, and therefore valuables should be kept under lock and key, and reasonable precautions should be taken not to leave temptation in the way of a chance passer-by. The best safeguard is for the church to be well used; and abroad very few precautions are found necessary. The people will gradually learn to use the church, if they are given the chance, and not prevented from saying their prayers by the churlishness of the parson. It is more important that the church should be open than that it should be adorned with valuable things. In some parishes voluntary watchers can be obtained; in others two or three old people can be provided with a pension as payment for a few hours' watch every day. Watchers should be instructed not to follow strangers about, nor to eye them suspiciously, nor to address them on the chance of tips.

Gothic architecture is most beautiful, when it is true, as the modern imitations of it hardly ever are; but it was only in use during four centuries of the Christian era, and is therefore not more ecclesiastical than other forms of architecture. In Gothic, as in all other times, the church builders simply used the current style that was in use for secular buildings as well. The parson should not try to tie down the architect to any popular ideas as to what is ecclesiastical—which is, indeed, just the reverse of the whole Gothic spirit. Shoddy Gothic is the most hideous of all architecture, because *corruptio optimi pessima*. In medieval, as in all other Christian times, architecture and all forms of decoration were free, although symbolism was so intensely appreciated. Even frontals and vestments were made without any regard to the supposed ecclesiastical character of their materials, birds, beasts, flowers, and heraldic devices being freely used.[6] Because the significance of symbolism was so well understood, sacred devices were used sparingly and with definite intention. Special 'ecclesiastical' materials only came in, even abroad, within living memory, and were due mainly to commercial reasons and the rage for cheapness.

Sound masonry is most necessary, even from the aesthetic point of view. A good architect's work is spoiled, if nothing is asked of the builder but a low tender; and the only advantage of this cheap building is that it tumbles down after twenty or thirty years, and so the world is rid of it.

Notes

1 This was long continued in many places. The Puritan Cartwright objected in 1573 that 'the minister sitteth in the chancel, with his back to the people.' Bishop Wren in 1636 appeals to post-Reformation practice in favour of this custom (*Parentalia*, 78). 40

2 The lights on the Rood-loft were allowed to remain by the Injunctions of 1538, when many other lights were forbidden. But the Injunctions of 1547 forbade all candles except the 'two lights upon the high altar, before the sacrament, which for the signification that Christ is the very true light of the world, they shall suffer to remain still.' If, therefore, these latter Injunctions can be shown to have the authority of Parliament, then the Rood-lights are not ornaments of the Rubric.

3 Works, ii. 4.

4 'At or near the church door, to signify that Baptism was the entrance into the Church mystical.'

5 As late as 1644 they were in use, for the Ordinance of the Puritan Parliament on May 9, 1644, orders 'that no Copes, Surplisses, superstitious Vestments, Roods or Roodlons or holy-water Fonts shall be or be any more used in any church or chapell within this

realm...and that all Copes, Surplisses, superstitious Vestments, Roods and Fonts aforesaid be likewise utterly defaced.' Scobell's Collection of Acts, 1644, p. 70.

6 *E.g.* the inventory of Lincoln Cathedral for 1536 enumerates the following designs worked on the vestments (they are tabulated by Mr. Macalister in his *Ecclesiastical Vestments*)'.—Leopards, harts, falcons, do. with crowns in their mouths, swans, ostriches, ostrich-feathers, popinjays, lions, owls, black eagles, peacocks, gryphons, dragons, phoenix. In addition to these are figures of the Divine Persons, incidents in the life of Christ, of our Lady and other Saints, figures of the Angels and Saints, and emblems such as roses and lilies, sun, moon and stars; also crowns, clouds, knots, inscriptions, initials, and heraldic devices.

CHAPTER II
THE ALTAR AND ITS FURNITURE

All altars should be 3 ft. 3 in. high, and *at least* deep enough to take a corporal 20 in. square, with an inch or two to spare. Their length will depend upon the dimensions and character of the church; and, as the whole dignity of effect depends very much upon the length of the altar, the advice of a competent architect should be sought. It should be borne in mind that altars are nearly always too short nowadays:[1] the vast majority of churches suffer greatly in this respect. As for the material of which the holy Table should be made, it may suffice to state that wooden altars were sometimes used before the Reformation, while many stone ones were set up in the eighteenth and early part of the nineteenth centuries in this country. *Plain* stone altars are by far the best.

The minimum amount of furniture allowed by the Canons of 1603 for the Lord's Table is (1) A frontal, 'a carpet of silk or other decent stuff,' and (2) 'A fair linen cloth at the time of the ministration.'[2] We are not, therefore, allowed to dispense with frontals. We may be grateful that the naked altar is not allowed by our Church, because this Puritan, French fashion helps to destroy that teaching power of the Church's seasons which needs so much to be enforced, and also because the element of colour is sadly lacking in modern churches both English and foreign.

The frontal, if accurately made with a backing of union cloth, needs no frame. It can be hung by rings from hooks under the altar-slab, without any rod or wooden lath; and it may be folded up when not in use. This seems to have been the general ancient custom. It dispenses with the need of a large chest; and most frontals look the better for not hanging stiffly. But for some embroidery a frame is necessary.

It is generally safer to avoid embroidery altogether. It is one of the most difficult and expensive of the arts, and nearly all so-called ecclesiastical work is thoroughly bad—fussy, vulgar, weak and ugly. If it is used at all it must be of the best, and the church-furnisher must be shunned. A real artist must be employed, otherwise the money spent will be worse than wasted.[3] Amateurs should not attempt embroidery, unless they have learned the art from a competent teacher (and there are few such); but the most effective stitch is a simple one, and therefore amateurs can usefully work under an artist who carries out the design and chooses the silks.

On the other hand, plain materials should not be used, but figured silks, or mixtures of silk and wool, etc. There are even one or two printed Morris chintzes which make beautiful frontals.

It requires experience as well as natural gifts to know how a material will work out when it is taken out of a shop and set up in the peculiar light of a church. To avoid disaster (and most frontals are nothing less than ecclesiastical calamities), amateurs should only attempt frontals under advice.

The frontal should have a fringe along the bottom, and preferably at the sides as well. For an average-sized altar the bottom fringe may be 3 in. deep, and that at the side 1 in. There may be strips of other material and colour on the frontal, but they are not necessary, and often the frontal is better without them.

The Frontlet (often mistakenly called the super-frontal) is a practical necessity for hiding the suspension of the frontal. For convenience it may always be red in colour, but any colour is admissible.[4] It is often made too deep. For an ordinary altar a depth of 7½ in., including fringe, or even less, is sufficient. The fringe should be about 1½ in., and laid on the frontlet, not hanging below it. The frontlet should *never* extend over the top of the altar: it should be tacked to one of the under linen cloths, like an apparel; but it is more convenient that the linen used for this purpose should be stout and of a dark-blue colour: such linen can be got at Morris's, or from Harris (Derwent Mills, Cockermouth), or that used for butchers' blouses will suffice. If the altar stand clear (as it should), the linen cloth can fall a couple of inches over the back, and leaden weights or an iron rod will keep the whole in position. If anything rest on the back of the altar, which is an objectionable foreign practice, then the method of fixing the cloth with drawing-pins (plugging a stone altar with wood for this purpose) seems to be unavoidable.

Altar Apparels add much to the beauty of the altar. They can be of any colour that suits the frontal and frontlet, and require, of course, taste in the selection of their material. They may hang 1 foot to 15 in. from the ground, and may be fixed with hook and eye to the top of the frontal: for an average altar 10 to 12 in. is wide enough. They should be fringed at the bottom, and have braid or narrow fringe at the sides.

The ecclesiastical devices on frontals, which one so often sees, are not in harmony with Catholic tradition. They are usually of a cast-iron, soulless, and altogether objectionable character; quite unlike the free and gorgeous designs they are supposed to imitate, as can be seen by a visit to the South Kensington and other museums.

The Linen Cloths. It is a very ancient custom that there should be three linen cloths on the top of the altar, the object no doubt being to provide against accidents with the chalice, as well as to secure a smooth and substantial surface. The dirty habit of making with the frontlet a permanent velvet cover to the altar is not to be commended.

The outer cloth (the 'fair linen' of the Canon) should be long enough to reach down to within a few inches of the ground at each end. It may have five crosses embroidered in linen thread on it,[5] as a quincunx, and it may also have embroidery at the ends, or it may be altogether plain. The ends may be fringed; but there is no English precedent for any lace on them. It may be exactly the width of the altar; and I think it looks better if none of it hang over the frontlet.

The two undercloths should be exactly the size of the top of the altar, and quite plain. One of them may, as we have seen, be tacked on to the frontlet. It is an ancient custom that no other material but linen shall cover the top of the altar.[6] The linen for altars should be stout: undercloths may be of diaper. The Roman fashion of tacking lace to one of these cloths is against all English tradition, and very seldom looks well. Anything suggestive of effeminacy should be rigidly excluded, the more so as it always has a tendency to creep in through the efforts of well-meaning women. The hem of the undercloths may be ¾ in., of the fair linen 1 in. at the sides and 2 in. at the ends.

It is cleaner to follow the old custom of removing the linen after service, especially the outer cloth of an altar which is not in daily use. It can be taken on to a wooden roller and put away in a drawer. In any case the Lord's Table should be protected by a cover. This cover should be exactly the same size as the *mensa*, unless the fair linen cloth is left on, in which case it may be 12 inches longer. It may be of silk (say a good yellow or green) lined with blue linen, or of blue linen lined with American cloth; in either case it would need a binding.

Whether gradines can be included among the ornaments allowed by the rubric is a disputed point. The majority of experts think that they were never in use here; and undoubtedly it was the general custom for the two candlesticks to be placed on the altar itself. But the gradine was sometimes used in England from the Jacobean period until the present day. Post-Reformation use can, therefore, be urged in its favour; and a shelf has something to recommend it, on the score of convenience alone, if it be low—say 3 in. in height. But anything like a flight of steps is unsightly. The altar should not look like a sideboard, and it cannot be too often remembered that the altar itself should be the central feature of a church and not any of its adjuncts. When a gradine is ugly or cold and irremovable, it can be redeemed by being entirely covered with a piece of really good tapestry, which of course need not be changed, except, perhaps, in Lent.

The Ornaments on the Altar included under the rubric are a cross or crucifix, cushions, and one or two candlesticks. Reliquaries, images, and plate were also formerly used for decking the altars. It was generally the custom to remove cross and candlesticks from the altar after service.

The Cross was very generally used, but not always, before the Reformation;[7] though nowadays many seem to consider it a necessity. In cases where a painting forms the altar-piece it is often better dispensed with, especially for minor altars; and the appropriateness of using a cross where the crucifixion forms part of the altar-piece is more than questionable. Although altar crucifixes are certainly included under the rubric, there is much to be said both from the ceremonial and from the theological point of view against their use on the altar.[8] The proper place for a representation of the crucified Redeemer is the Rood-screen. In any case the primitive crucifix, in which our Lord is represented in an attitude of benediction and majesty, is more seemly than the twisted and distorted figure one often sees.

The Candlesticks. The use of a row of six candlesticks above the altar is pure Romanism, and cannot be defended from our rubric. An altar with two candlesticks only is more dignified and more beautiful. Furthermore, a row of candles hides the altar-piece, which should be one of the most rich and beautiful things in the church; the miserable way in which priceless masterpieces are hidden in Italian churches by tall candlesticks and tawdry sham flowers will be painfully familiar to every traveller.

Many people have been misled by the Sarum custom which orders eight candles for the greater festivals. But six of these candles stood round about the altar and only two were on it: this represents the utmost to which even a gorgeous cathedral like Salisbury went in the matter of altar-lights.[9] Another cause of error was the *sex in eminencia coram reliquiis et crucifixo et ymaginibus ibi constitutis* of the Consuetudinary; but these six were for the rood, and not altar-lights at all, nor in any way connected with a shelf or gradine. The local medieval rules of Salisbury Cathedral are not in the least binding on us; and the increase in the number of lights at festivals should depend upon the size and richness of the church.[10]

There is no authority whatever for reserving special candles for use at Mass, and no such things as 'Vesper lights' are known to the Church.

Tall candles are a modern fashion, and often spoil the look of a church. The height both of candles and candlesticks is a matter of proportion for the architect to decide. For many years after the Reformation candlesticks were made low and broad even on the Continent. If stocks have to be used they look all the better for being plain and short. If covered with wax their surface soon assumes a disagreeable appearance: it is better in my opinion to enamel them, socket and all, with wax-colour paint. Metal sockets break the line of the candle; and trumpery shields are really detestable. Coloured stocks are generally as bad. Indeed nothing can be more beautiful than the white line of a moderately thick candle. To use no stock but to burn the candle to within a few inches of the end is the more excellent way, and is possible with all well-proportioned candlesticks, more especially on minor altars. Much of the beauty of a lighted candle is due to the glow which the flame throws into the few inches of candle nearest the wick; therefore, for this, if for no other reason, sham tin candles with springs inside should be consigned to the dust-heap. The Church has never sanctioned the use of anything but real wax for candles; semi-transparent composition candles are therefore irregular as well as ugly. Furthermore, the ends and scrapings of real wax candles can always be sold back to the chandler. If all the altar candles are made of the same diameter, they can be used up, when burnt short, at the minor altars.

It is always better to get a few good things than many bad ones. It is also better for poor churches to buy a good thing in simple material than a bad thing in more expensive material. For instance, if standard candlesticks are wanted cheap, they can be turned in deal and painted a good colour, or stained green, for two or three pounds. But if metal ones are wanted, a good price must be paid and a skilled craftsman employed. A proper craftsman can be obtained through the Clergy and Artists' Association, the Art Worker's Guild,[11] or the Guilds of Handicraft.[12] For altar use, also, wooden candlesticks can be turned and painted or gilt, where economy is an object. Standards should be weighty, and about 5 ft. high (not counting the stock): if there are two only, they should stand on the pavement in front of the steps, and well beyond the line of the altar on either side.

Cushions were generally used for supporting the missal, and they are still ordered by the Roman rubrics. Desks, however, were not unknown: wood is perhaps better for this purpose than brass, which is cold to the hand and scratches the book; and it should be covered with a strip of silk brocade or tapestry of any good colour, which should be long enough to cover the desk and hang nearly to the bottom behind. As cushions survived in the English Church through all the bad times, it seems a pity to drop them now. They are extremely convenient; and, if made of beautiful material, they add a pleasant touch of colour and warmth to the general effect. Two is the most convenient number, as it lessens the amount to be carried by the server. The cushions can be left at either end of the altar out of service time. Very rich ones may be provided with an extra (but not ugly) cover to protect them from the dust,—blue linen is a good material. The size will depend on the altar-book. The cushions should be stuffed with down (not too tightly), and made up with cord in the usual way. They may have tassels.

The Books for the altar may include the Book of Common Prayer (with which may be bound up any special collects, epistles, and gospels allowed by the Ordinary), and the Gospels and Epistles bound up separately. Four or five silk markers are a convenience in the altar-book, and so are tags gummed to the pages at the beginning of the Service, at the Creed, and from the Consecration to the end of the Service. The latter tags are generally put in missals, but that at the beginning is almost as useful, while that at the Creed is very necessary to save fumbling about when the Gospel is finished.

The custom of using two embroidered markers, which are changed with the seasons, is a piece of fancy ritual which does not improve the condition of the book. I have found that the most convenient and least destructive plan is to have three or four rather narrow markers (about half-inch) sewn into the binding, and each of a different colour (say yellow, red, blue, and green). That for the colour of the service (using yellow for white, which would become dirty) is turned across the page, before the book is set on the altar; and, if there are to be any extra collects, other markers are turned across the pages that contain them.

Flower vases are of late introduction, and therefore not strictly covered by our rubric; though flowers themselves are a very ancient feature in church decoration. But now that flowers are usually preserved in water, there can be little objection to their being placed in vases, *if they are removed after a day or two.* Anything like decaying vegetable matter, with its taint and slime, or wormy flower-pots should of course not be tolerated near God's Board.

Still it must be remembered that, in these days when many people are occupied about our altars, the tendency is always to lose simplicity; and the loss of simplicity is the destruction of dignity. A great deal of money is usually wasted on flowers, which ought to be spent on necessary ornaments. Flowers are not necessities of worship, beautiful as they are; and they can easily be overdone. The idea that there must be flowers on the altar except in Advent and Lent should be discouraged. Where they are used it seems best to let them be the free offering of the people, and not to buy them. Their only traditional use is for festivals. The altar ought to be rich and beautiful in itself, and not to *need* flowers to make it pleasant to the eye. In private houses, desolate wall-papers cause people (generally without knowing why) to cover their walls with fans and fal-lals. In the same way ladies often unconsciously try to atone for a blatant frontal, or to cover a chilly reredos, by a crowd of flowers. It will not do. If the altar is not beautiful and dignified before a single ornament is set on it, nothing will make it so. Indeed the general use of Christendom has been not to set any ornaments on the altar except at service time.

A certain ugly shape of brass vase (decorated with sacred emblems at a slightly higher cost) has become almost an article of faith in some churches. The use of plain glass vases will help to remove the hard effect produced by these brazen jars; and so will good earthenware, such as can be got in some old-fashioned towns, and at one or two shops, like Mr. De Morgan's in Great Marlborough Street. By far the best glass is that made by the Whitefriars Company (Powell's), Whitefriars Street, E.C. Tin shapes to hold flowers need only be mentioned to be condemned. Flowers should be arranged lightly, freely, and gracefully. Intelligent people hardly need reminding that, if flowers are used, there is no conceivable reason why they should follow the colour of the frontal, or be tortured into emblematic shapes.

There is no authority and no need for altar cards.

Of the Reredos little need be said here, as it is a concern of the architect. There is no part on which the richest colour is more needed than here, and really beautiful reredoses could be made for a quarter the cost of the badly carved, uncoloured stonework which defaces many of our churches and cathedrals. The simple upper frontal of silk or wool tapestry[13] forms the cheapest, and for many churches the most effective, backing to the altar. It can be of the same size as the lower frontal, and should not obscure the east window; it may be changed with the seasons. High dorsels and canopies should not be attempted without professional advice.[14] Canopies, when they are used, should always project over the altar as well as over the candles.

Wings, or Riddels as they were called, should as a rule project at right angles to the wall, and reach as far as the front of the altar. The rods should be strong, so as not to bend in the slightest degree with the weight of the curtains: wrought iron is a better and stronger material than brass, and cannot tarnish. The rods may have sconces for candles at their ends, and these may be of a brighter metal, in which case they should be lacquered. Sometimes the riddels were hung between four pillars which stood at the four corners of the altar,—an excellent arrangement. The curtains should not be of a shabby material or washy in colour, as they generally are.

The Tables of the Ten Commandments ordered by the Canons were not unknown in pre-Reformation days. In Elizabeth's reign they stood over the Lord's Table; but since 1603 the 'east end of every church' of Canon 82 seems most literally followed by a table on either side of the chancel arch at the east end of the nave, because the place must be 'where the people may best see and read the same.' In these days of universal education and cheap prayer books there is no need for the tables to be large. The lettering may be made very beautiful by an artist, 'to give some comely ornament,' as the Queen said.

Credence tables may not have been in use in 1548, but they were used here in the seventeenth century by Andrewes, Laud, and their school, and the secular courts have agreed that they are required for the reception of the elements until the alms have been presented.[15] The *locus administrationis* of the Sarum rubric may have been a credence. It was used by the monastic orders. The credence should be on the south side of the altar, and, *if there is room*, against the south and not the east wall. It is seemly to cover it with a linen cloth, but there is no English authority for placing candles upon it.

Now that the services are in English it is considered by some that the use of the small sacring bell inside the church is unnecessary. Where it is used care should be taken that it be not of too shrill a tone.

There is very little evidence for the use of a tabernacle in England, where the general method of reservation was in the hanging pyx,[16] which was suspended over the high altar. It is believed by some that aumbries have also been used for this purpose.

Lamps can be hung before altars. One or three are generally enough. Pure olive oil should always be used: and there should be a little water at the bottom of the glass. Floating wicks are most convenient.

Altar-rails were introduced by Archbishop Laud's school to protect the altars against irreverence and to prevent their removal. Though sometimes extremely useful, they are, therefore, not binding upon us. Often they are very much in the way, as architects are apt to place them too near the Holy Table, and to make the entrance too small. In some cases they can be moved to a more convenient distance, in others they can more advantageously be replaced by movable wooden benches (which were sometimes used before and during the sixteenth century). Often two short benches at the side for infirm people will suffice, as it is not difficult for a hale person to kneel upright for a few moments without assistance. As the altar is now generally protected by a chancel screen or gates, the rails are no longer needed as they were in the eighteenth century. When they are used, it will save the clergy many an aching back if the architect is told not to place them close against the step, so as to force the communicants to kneel on a lower level than that on which the ministers stand.

A linen Houseling Cloth was held under the communicants or laid on the bench at the time of the Rubric, and for long after; indeed at Wimborne Minster it is still in use at the present day. Three feet is a convenient width, and its length will be as long as the rails, to which it may be fastened by hooks.

The Piscina is a necessity. It enables the water that has been used for rinsing the purificators, etc., to be reverently disposed of. It should of course be kept scrupulously clean, and the drain should run on to the soil outside. The shelf, which is sometimes found above it, is for the cruets, etc., to stand on.

The Sedilia should be hung with some good material which may continue over the seats and reach to within two or three inches of the ground. Cushions may be placed on the seats, and where the hangings only reach to the seats they are a necessity. Small chairs or stools will also be necessary for the servers, and where there are no structural sedilia chairs also for the ministers, but these should be of such a shape that the vestments can easily fall over the back. In building a new church it is best for the seats in the sedilia to be movable.

The Carpets are far too important a factor in the colour scheme of a church to be left to individual whims: they should be chosen under advice. Good Turkey carpets are becoming scarcer every year; but those at Morris's are beautiful and most durable, and the advice there may be relied upon. Some of the big furnishers also supply good carpets now. Besides the carpet in front of the altar it is often advisable to spread other carpets or matting on the pavement or *planum* to prevent the danger of the ministers slipping: in this way, too, glaring tiles can often be advantageously hidden. In the case of poor churches it is useful to remember that felt can easily be procured of good colours; and, though it is only a substitute, it is far better than a bad carpet, for the average commercial carpet has no real colour at all, and is little more durable than felt.

Flat cushions or mats for the servers are a convenience, and should be provided for each server at every point where he will have to kneel, at least unless there is a carpet. But nothing of the kind is required for the priest; the foot-pace or predella where he stands should be covered only by the carpet. The mat which one sometimes sees in the midst of the foot-pace is a great nuisance, and has come down only as a relic of the hassock when the priest knelt at the north end.

Notes

1 The old altar at Arundel is 12½ ft. by 4.

2 Canon 82.57

3 The Clergy and Artists' Association (6 Millbank Street, S. W.) will recommend good embroiderers and teachers; Morris (449 Oxford Street, W.) also.

4 *E.g.* in the Exhumation of St. Hubert at the National Gallery there is a beautiful green frontal with purple apparels and frontlet.

5 In the instances given by Mr. Atchley (*S.P.E.S. Trans.* iv. 3) there are not only crosses of silk on altar-cloths, but also black crosses, 'fflour-de-lusis and crownyz with 5 red-crossis thereon and J H S in the middis,' another 'with 3 part blew starres,' another with '3 blew kayes at each end,' another with 'blew kayes' in the middle, another with I H S in red silk in two places.

6 There were many exceptions to this in the way of undercloths, such as a cloth of 'hair.' But the use of a cere-cloth is extremely doubtful. (See Mr. Atchley in *S.P.E.S. Trans.* iv. 3.) Horsehair is apt to breed fungi. Cotton is to be avoided.

7 After the Reformation, high churchmen often set crosses or crucifixes on the altar; and Queen Elizabeth's crucifix is famous. In the eighteenth century the great Bishop Butler had a plain marble cross let into wall over the altar in his chapel; but crucifixes had quite fallen into disuse,—in spite of their prominence in the Lutheran churches.

8 Rev. F. E. Brightman, *S.P.E.S. Trans.* iii. 105.

9 Mr. Comper in *S.P.E.S.* iii. 204, and iv. 75. *Alcuin Tract*, ii. 31. See also on the subject of lights, Chapter V of this book.

10 In the Sarum Customary, a *parochial* book (just published by Mr. Frere, p. 4), all the directions in the cathedral Consuetudinary as to the number of lights are *omitted*.

11 The address of the Art Worker's Guild is Clifford's Inn Hall, E.C.

12 There is a Guild of Handicraft at Birmingham, and one at Essex House, Mile End Road, E.

13 The tapestries which William Morris designed are by far the most beautiful that have been produced in modern times. They can be got at 449 Oxford Street. There are some good ones also at Watts', 30 Baker Street, W.

14 High dorsels are adaptations to particular needs of the upper frontal, which with its riddels is the normal furniture of the altar, and represents the ciborium curtains of the basilica. The riddels should be the same height as the upper frontal, i.e. about 6½ ft. from the ground. They should not be spread out unless they are very high.

15 *Book of Church Law*, 99.

16 Described by Mr. Comper in *S.P.E.S. Trans.* iv. 80-5.

CHAPTER III
COLOURS, VESTMENTS, AND ORNAMENTS

1. Liturgical Colours.—It will clear the ground if we consider first the question of colours. Although there is still great confusion on this subject, and almost universal misunderstanding, the question is, in the light of recent research, a simple one, and one also about which the experts are agreed. The following axioms may with safety be dogmatically stated—

(1.) The colours used should be those which were in use at the time specified by the Ornaments Rubric. The Prayer Book does not refer us to the earliest sequence (or fragment of a sequence) that we can find, but to the year 1548-9.

(2.) The colours generally used at that time were the white, red, violet, green, and black sequence, which is again most commonly used in England at the present day, with the addition of yellow or green for Confessors and of red for Passiontide.

(3.) At the same time there was never anything like a rigid uniformity; exceptions of every kind abound in the inventories; and poor churches were not expected to have a complete suite of vestments; nor have the special 'shades' of colour sometimes advocated any authority beyond that of certain ecclesiastical shops.

It will be obvious at once to the reader that ignorance of the above facts has led to two very unfortunate errors. On the one hand some clergy, through a laudable desire to be faithful to English tradition, have attempted to revive the local Salisbury use, and thus have considerably puzzled both themselves and the faithful. Some clergy, on the other hand, offended by the want of clearness of the so-called Sarum use, have adopted the white-red-green-violet sequence; but, misled by the claims of the Salisbury ritualists, have thought that in so doing they were committing themselves to Rome. Incredible as it may seem, these loyal Anglicans adopted the word 'Roman use,' and believing themselves committed to Roman Catholicism in externals they took as their pattern the modern developments of that Church, and came to neglect with a most strange persistency those things which are ordered by lawful authority. The result has been a widespread spirit of lawlessness in the Church, which has alienated many faithful churchmen, made the winning of those outside more difficult, and given some show of justice and some measure of power to those who attack the Catholic basis of the Church of England. In a word, it has made the Church appear ridiculous to the average layman, to the Dissenter, to the Agnostic, and certainly not least to the Roman Catholic.

Unfortunately, too, while the Ornaments Rubric refers us to all that was best and most beautiful in ecclesiastical tradition, the present Roman Catholic customs and ornaments represent the lowest pitch to which the decline of art and craftsmanship, and the growth of the commercial spirit, have ever reduced religious ceremonial.

No doubt, had the word Sarum never been introduced, the loyal Anglican clergy would have used the words English Use, and the hitherto untried plan of honestly obeying the Prayer Book would have become general, to the honour of the Church and the confusion of her enemies. The misfortune was that the clergy thought they must either be 'Sarum' or 'Roman,' and the many difficulties of the former use drove them, as they thought, to the latter.

Putting on one side the peculiar customs of modern Rome as out of the question for every man who has taken vows of obedience to the Prayer Book, let me point out why the so-called Sarum use is also undesirable, (1.) The Prayer Book does not refer us to the diocese of Salisbury of the fourteenth century, but to the England of the sixteenth. (2.) No one knows what the Sarum use as to colours was for Advent, Christmas, Epiphany, Lent, Ascensiontide, Whitsuntide, and Trinity Sunday; consequently the so-called Sarum uses are really one-half made up from the fancy of nineteenth-century ritualists. (3.) The common idea is that only those four colours which are casually mentioned in the Sarum books were used,—white, red, yellow, and (in some MSS.) black. But the inventories show that in Salisbury cathedral itself there were in 1222 vestments of *Violette, Purpurea, de Serico Indico* (of blue silk); in 1462 altar-cloths of purple, blue and black, white and blue, chasubles of purple and blue, altar-cloths and vestments of red and green; in 1536, three green copes and five chasubles, with tunicles, etc., of green; while the inventories, taken in the very year *2nd Edward VI.*, to which our Rubric refers us, give the vestments of the chantries in the cathedral as of 'white, red, blue, green, black, purple, motley, of blue black and white combined, and "braunched of dyverse colours," with white for Lent.'[1]

It is clear, then, that those colours, violet and green, which are commonly thought to be peculiarly Roman were actually included in the Sarum use of the sixteenth century, and violet and blue, at least, in that of the thirteenth.

As it is impossible to tell how these colours were used at Salisbury, owing to the imperfect information of the books, we are forced to go to those dioceses where the order was set down more completely and distinctly. We have this more complete information in the case of the following dioceses,—Lichfield, Wells, Exeter, London, and Canterbury. The latest of these—the nearest, that is, to the time of the Ornaments Rubric—are the Pontificals of London (1406-26) and of Canterbury (1414-43); and the only complete ones are those of Exeter, London, and Canterbury, which were set forth by the bishops of the time. The London inventories show that the Pontifical was generally followed, but all inventories show a considerable amount of local variation.

Now, Exeter agrees almost exactly with London and Canterbury (which are identical), and curiously enough, both agree very nearly with *what is known* of the Sarum use (though not with the fancy 'Sarum use' which nineteenth-century theorists have compiled). The only important variation is that at Salisbury (as at Wells) red is given from Trinity to Advent,[2] instead of green (though the mention of green in the later inventories seems to show that Salisbury may have come round to the general use). If we put these uses together, therefore, supplementing what is wanting in the Sarum use by what was ordered in the Pontificals, we get the use which I have called *English*, with the exception that red was used for the Sundays after Trinity and Holy Innocents Day, and white for Pentecost. If we go further, and prefer the Pontificals because they are of a date nearer to that of the Ornaments Rubric—which is the most reasonable course—we shall substitute green for the Sarum red of the Trinity season; and even here we shall very likely not be departing from the actual custom at the Salisbury of 1548.

Thus we arrive at a sequence that was in national use at the time of the Ornaments Rubric, and was authoritative; and yet we have not departed from what is known of the actual use of Sarum in anything but the use of violet for the Innocents and red for Pentecost, if we retain the Sarum Passiontide red, which is allowed by the Pontificals. This sequence, too, differs but very slightly from the Roman sequence which is so well known at the present day. So closely have the issues been narrowed down by recent investigation!

If, instead of starting from Sarum, as I have here done for the sake of argument, we take our stand upon the Pontificals, which is by far the safer course, we can have no hesitation whatever in deciding upon violet for the Holy Innocents, red for Pentecost, and instead of the Sarum 'Sunday' red we shall use the far more intelligible and more convenient green; and shall have the option of continuing the violet through Passiontide.

While allowing the optional use of violet for Passiontide (which is an obvious convenience in the case of poor churches), I would plead for the use of red (with black or dark blue orphreys and apparels for preference) at this season on these grounds. (1.) It is more in accordance with liturgical propriety to change the colours at Passiontide: every diocese except that of Rome formerly did so. (2.) It is more instructive to the people, and a most useful and beautiful enrichment of the colour sequence. (3.) The Pontificals do not insist upon violet; they only say that it is to be used 'till Maundy Thursday, *or, according to some churches, till Passion Sunday.*' (4.) The Exeter sequence, which is so close to the Pontificals, also gives violet up 'to Maundy Thursday, *or, according to some, until Passion Sunday.*' Later, in mentioning red it says, 'according to some, within Passion week (and on Maundy Thursday if the bishop does not celebrate) red must be used,' and again, 'on Maundy Thursday, when the Bishop consecrates the chrism, white, otherwise red.' (5.) Salisbury, Lichfield, and Wells all order red only. (6.) The inventories prove that red was still so used in the sixteenth century.

This sequence of the Pontificals and of Exeter, clear, complete, and authoritative as it is, has the additional practical advantage of being nearly identical with the sequence which obtains almost everywhere to-day.[3]

Fortunately, the English colour-sequence which I am describing can be obtained by every one in Dr. Legg's Churchman's Oxford Calendar (Mowbray, 1s.) and in the small penny Calendar published by the same firm. The only alterations I would in all humility suggest are the use of yellow instead of green for Confessors, and of the Passiontide red (with black apparels and orphreys). These would not, I think, be objected to by the compiler.[4]

Yellow seems to be a better colour for Confessors than green, as it is more generally understood; to use green for Confessors in Trinity-tide, for instance, is sadly confusing, now that green is everywhere understood as the ferial colour. Liturgically the question is unimportant, as yellow and green were regarded as interchangeable. Our latest Pontificals (London and Canterbury) order yellow; and, as they agree in this with Salisbury as well as with Exeter (though the latter allows green as an alternative), we are following the most general authority in preferring yellow. Among the dioceses mentioned above, the only exceptions are Wells (blue *and* green), and Lichfield (*varius*, a word of uncertain meaning).

The use of white for Lent was practically universal in the sixteenth century and earlier. It was generally of plain stuff, fustian, linen, or canvas, with crosses, roses, or other devices of red or blue. But it is nowhere ordered, and seems to have been simply a popular custom. It is therefore not binding on us, though allowable; but as its revival now would be a very unpopular custom, confusing the much-tried layman, who naturally associates a dark colour with Lent, I submit that it has little chance of obtaining amongst us, and that its introduction would only increase the present confusion.

The 'violet' for Lent does not of course mean the unpleasant colour (so remote from the colour of the violet flower) at present provided by the shops. There is no such restriction as to tints, and dark blue or purple is equally suitable for Lent. It may be mentioned here that there is not a single authority —in the Sarum books or elsewhere— for the use of red either in Lent (except in Passiontide) or Advent.[5]

Here is the colour-sequence ordered in the latest Pontificals, those of London and Canterbury (1406-26, and 1414-43). The principal variants of other dioceses are given in brackets. — *Advent*, violet or purple: *Christmas*, white: *St. Stephen*, red: *St. John Evan.*, white; *H. Innocents*, violet (Exeter, and all others, red): *Circumcision*, white: *Epiphany*, white: *Ep. oct. to Septuagesima*, green: *Septuagesima to Passion Sunday*, violet or purple: 'according to some churches' the use of violet is allowed by the Pontificals to stop on Passion Sunday. (*Passion Sunday to Easter Eve*, Salisbury, Lichfield, Wells, red.) *Palm Sunday*, violet or purple (Exeter, violet or red): *Maundy Thurs.* white (Exeter, white or red): *Good Friday*, black (Exeter, violet or red): *Eastertide*, white: *Rogations*, violet or purple: *Ascensiontide*, white: *Whitsuntide*, red: *Trinity*, white (Exeter, green or white): *Trinity to Advent*, green (Salisbury and Wells, red): *Feasts of B.V.M., Nativ. John Bap., Michaelmas*, white: *St. Mary Mag.*, yellow: *All Saints*, white (Exeter, red and white, or all colours): *Apostles, Martyrs, Evangelists*, red (all the English sequences have red for Evangelists as against the Roman white): *Confessors*, yellow (Exeter, yellow or green, Wells,

blue and green, Salisbury, yellow; none have white): *Requiem*, black
(Exeter, black and violet).

To this it may be added that the colour for Dedication Festivals has
everywhere been white.

2. Vestments.—With regard to all ornaments and vestments one
precaution is most necessary. The parson must make it clearly
understood that he will not accept a single thing for the church
unless the advice has first been sought of that person who overlooks
the decoration of the church. Who that person is will depend on
circumstances, but he must be a competent judge; and committees
are useless unless their members are modest.

If this precaution is not taken the services of the church are certain in
time to be vulgarised. Some kind friend will work an impossible
stole; another will compose a ruinous frontal, and, without warning
any one, present it as a pleasant surprise when it is finished; another
will be attracted by some brass-work of the gilt-gingerbread order in
a shop-window, and with a smile of kindly triumph will deposit it
one day in the vestry. It will be too late then for the parson to protest:
all these good people will be hurt (and one cannot blame them) if
their presents are rejected. But if it be publicly explained beforehand
that beauty of effect is a most difficult task, for which a life-long
training is required—and that a church must suffer if left to the
chance of a multitude of individual tastes, this catastrophe will be
avoided.

Sometimes one is tempted to think that folk consider anything good
enough for a church. But this is not generally the case. It simply is
that the elements of artistic knowledge have not yet entered the
heads of many people,—and will not, unless the Church educate
them by its example. Simplicity, unity, proportion, restraint, richness
of colour, ecclesiastical propriety,[6] these things are simply not
understood by a vast number. It is not their fault; they have had no
opportunity of learning: they want to help the church, and they will
do so well if they are only taught; but, if not, it will not cross their
minds that decoration without harmony is just as excruciating as
music without harmony.

When a parson has no ear he generally has the wisdom to put the
music under good advice. It should be just the same when he has no
eye. He must remember that those who have not this defect will be
driven from the church by faults which to them offend not only

against the eye, but against the heart and intellect as well. If the vulgarities both in music and other forms of art, with which nearly every church is at present soiled, do not soon pass away, the quiet alienation of the most educated sections of the community will have gone too far for recovery.

The vestments worn by authority of Parliament in the year to which we are referred were—the cassock, surplice, hood, tippet or scarf, cap (choral cope), the albe and amice with their apparels, girdle, stole, maniple, chasuble, cope, dalmatic and tunicle, humeral veil, the rochet, the verger's gown.[7]

The Cassock in its English traditional form is double-breasted without buttons down the front, and kept in position by a broad sash. In this form it was worn (generally with the gown) as the usual out-door dress of the English clergy down to the beginning of the present century;[8] and in this form it still survives, somewhat attenuated, in the bishop's 'apron,' and in those churches where the preaching gown is used. The usual medieval shape seems to have been more single-breasted, with two or more buttons above the waist, but with none below; in fact, like the coat now worn by the boys of Christ's Hospital; and in some brasses the cassock is belted with a buckled strap. It was very like that worn by civilians; and the clergy seem to have used what they found convenient, with some regard to the usual out-door dress of the period. Nowadays cassocks with buttons down the front are often worn; but neither beauty nor convenience is gained by the excessive number of buttons that one sometimes sees, and the buttons, unless they are made flat, are apt to stick into the knees. Now that the civilian's dress is shortened it seems hardly incumbent on the clergy always to wear their cassocks. But on the way to church, in the schools, at confirmations, at clerical meetings, there can be no reason for ignoring Canon 74, which orders the clergy 'usually' to wear the cassock, and with it the cap and gown, a beautiful dress. On state occasions the hood and tippet should also be worn.

Some sort of girdle or cincture has been long in use. The traditional shape since the time of Laud has been that of a broad band of black material. A short cloth band may be fastened with three buttons. A long sash had better be tied in a simple knot at the left side.

The Surplice. The pre-Reformation surplice, like that which has continued in use down to our own time, was very long and full.[9] To the mimicry of Rome which has obtained in some quarters we owe the short garment that is now sometimes seen, undignified and ungraceful. To wear a thing of this sort is scarcely to obey the Ornaments Rubric; it is as if a boy should wear a bathing-costume at a cricket match when he was told to wear a suit of flannels.

The surplice should fall to within about six inches of the ground, or to the ankles; and at the very shortest—by way of transition— nothing should be tolerated that is not well below the knee. It may be mentioned here that men are apt to think their surplices longer than they really are, because, when one leans forward to look at the length of the garment, it drops several inches in front.

A further cause that has led to the gradual cutting down of garments is the rage for cheapness, and the desire of the tailor to save as much material as possible. Before vestments became a commercial article, they remained full, on the Continent as well as here. Now the worship of Mammon has so far intrenched on the honour due to God that the sweater has his own way with us, and it is considered seemly for a minister to appear in church in the garment called a 'sausage-skin,' a so-called surplice that is not only short, but is entirely deprived of gathers, so that a few extra halfpence may be saved from the cost of worship.

Smocking has plenty of precedent for surplices. But it is not in the least necessary, while shape *is*. As for fulness, the most beautiful surplice (that like those represented on medieval monuments) will have a circumference of about 4½ yards. Surplices should never button in the front.[10] The most graceful sleeves hang down within a few inches of the skirt-hem, and are turned back over the hands; for preaching it will generally be found more convenient to use a surplice with sleeves that, while hanging nearly as low, do not extend beyond the wrist at the top.

It need hardly be said at the present time that there is no English precedent for the use of lace. It simply destroys all beauty of drapery in any garment upon which it is placed. Every artist will realise how much this means. Indeed, to the credit of our fellow-Christians on the Continent it must be said that they are rapidly discarding the use of lace, and with it that most indecent garment the cotta, which is fortunately not one of the vestments ordered by our Rubric. The ancient monastic orders have always retained, and still use, the full surplice.

The parson will therefore use a gentle authority against the good ladies who unconsciously try to approximate church vestments to the feminine attire with which they are familiar. For ecclesiastical vestments are for men, and it will be a bad day for us when we forget this fact. Of all the many vestments used at different times in the Church a well-cut surplice is perhaps the most beautiful.

The Hood has come down to us by custom, and its origin is obscure. None the less it clearly belongs to the ornaments of our Rubric, for the Prayer Book of 1549 shows that it was well established in its academical form at that time,—graduates, it says, may use in quire 'such hood as pertaineth to their several degrees, which they have taken in any university within this realm.'[11] Considering the conservatism of university authority, we may safely assume that the distinctive varieties of the academical hood were no new thing in 1549. Canon 58 orders it for all the clergy who have a degree, as well as the surplice.

A caution is necessary against the attempts sometimes made by tailors to reconstruct ancient shapes of the hood out of their own fancies. The idea that buttons should be used is especially unfounded. The only safe course is to take the hood in its traditional shape as it is; if it does not draggle down too far at the back, and if it shows a little of its substance (not a piece of mere tape) in front, its comeliness and convenience cannot I think be improved. As for its length, I would venture to suggest as a good criterion both of comfort and proportion that it should barely touch the seat when the wearer is sitting down.

Some high-church clergy seem to have inherited the Puritan dislike to the hood, discarding it, in defiance both of authority and tradition. A century and a half ago this dislike of the hood was, more appropriately, the mark of a section of the low-church clergy.

The almuce need only be mentioned here, as its place was taken by the hood and tippet. Originally a fur hood and cape combined, with long pendants in front, such as was much needed in the days when churches were very cold, it was replaced by the tippet or scarf, which was first of black material lined or edged with fur, then of black silk only.[12] The furred scarf was reserved for dignitaries, as it might be still.

The Tippet or Black Scarf. The old meaning of the word tippet has hardly yet died out; there are many clergymen of the Church of

Ireland who can still remember hearing the ecclesiastical scarf called a tippet. It is so defined in Bailey's Dictionary (1761). It would be a great pity to let the old meaning go; because the Canons on the subject must be misunderstood when the modern foreign idea of a short cape is read into the word tippet. 'The tippet,' says the Alcuin Club tract on the Ornaments Rubric,[13] 'was a scarf generally of black silk, sometimes lined with fur.'

There is no known authority for confining the use of the tippet to dignitaries and chaplains: that custom grew up in the days when the direction of the canons as to copes also fell into abeyance, and is paralleled by the general disuse of the hood among the parish clergy at the same time.[14] There is plenty of evidence that the use of the tippet was enforced upon the clergy by the Bishops from the time of Elizabeth to that of Charles II., and was much opposed by the Puritans, who hated the cap and tippet as much as they hated the surplice. If in the light of this known contemporary practice we read Canon 58, which orders the tippets of non-graduates to be made of *stuff*, and Canon 74, which, dealing with the walking dress of the clergy, orders Masters of Arts holding any ecclesiastical living, not less than Doctors and Dignitaries, to wear both hoods and tippets of *silk* or sarsenet, we cannot avoid the conclusion that the tippet should be worn by all the clergy—of stuff by non-graduates (and presumably also by Bachelors), of silk by Masters and those above that degree.

The free use of black is so necessary to the beauty of all public services (a fact which artists well know, though it is generally forgotten by others) that the common substitution of coloured stoles for tippets is the more to be regretted. There is no authority, English or Continental, for the use of the stole in choir, while the black scarf or tippet has come down to us from before the Reformation, and the authority for its use is unmistakable.

The tippet should be worn outside the hood. The stitched gathers at the neck are a modern corruption of the tailors; besides spoiling the folds, they make the tippet wear out quickly. The tippet should be made of a piece of silk (or for non-graduates, cashmere or merino) long enough to fall within two inches of the bottom of the surplice, and from 13 to 19 in. broad, so that, when it is folded double and tacked, it forms a flat band from 6 to 9 in. broad. If the material be thin and soft, it may be even broader, and will need an interlining. The ends may be pinked (in zig-zags) with a pair of scissors, without any use of the needle. The tippet should be kept folded up flat; and a twist at the neck into three folds, in putting it on, will cause it to hang as it should. Those clergy who feel the cold will do well to have a tippet interlined with thick wool for winter wear.

The Cap, or 'square cap,' may have had its origin in the almuce. For the almuce was originally used to cover the head, and when it ceased to fulfil that function the cap seems to have been introduced. It has gone through several modifications: once of the comely shape that we see in the portraits of Bishop Fox and others, it developed in the seventeenth century into the form sometimes called the Canterbury cap (of limp material, with a tuft on the top), and then into the still beautiful college-cap in England, and abroad into the positively ugly biretta. There is no conceivable reason for English churchmen to discard their own shape in favour of a foreign one, except that the biretta offends an immense number of excellent lay folk, and thus makes the recovery of the Church more difficult.

English tradition since the Reformation has been against the wearing of any head-dress except the coif in church, from motives of reverence; and nowadays, when churches are heated, there is no need for anything but a skull-cap for those whose heads are sensitive. Canon 18 orders that 'No man shall cover his head in the church or chapel in the Divine Service, except he have some infirmity, in which case let him wear a night-cap or coif.' The well-known picture of the Seven Sacraments by Van der Weyden at Antwerp shows that in Flanders at any rate the coif was in general use at all kinds of services in the fifteenth century.

The biretta is a secular headgear as well as the college-cap; vergers and choristers wear it in France, and so do barristers. The Canterbury cap is on the other hand distinctively ecclesiastical as well as English; its shape seems now to be tending to the more compact older form; and, as our superiors have largely adopted it, there are good reasons for the parson to wear it with his cassock and for outdoor processions, unless he wears the college-cap.

The Ornaments Rubric certainly does not cover the ceremonial use of a cap (still less of a biretta) at Mass. A cap was however used in choir (where there were many cutting draughts) and for processions. Some modern ritualists have given directions for the management of the biretta at Mass; but their footnotes will show that they have had to go for their authority, not to traditional sources, but to Le Vavasseur's edition of *Baldeschi*.

The Choral Cope was no doubt also used for the sake of warmth: indeed, with this garment worn over the ample fur almuce, surplice, and cassock, the medieval parson must have been well muffled up. It was black, being often called the *cappa nigra*, and was more like a sleeveless gown than a stiff cope. Old effigies and brasses show that it fell gracefully from the shoulders to the heels, almost covering the arms. There does not seem to be any evidence of its use in parish churches, though it very likely was used in them. It is almost obsolete, perhaps because its protection in church came to be less needed. Its use for funerals and out-door processions in bad weather would save some washing and a few lives. Perhaps the short black cape (sometimes mistakenly called a 'tippet') which is worn by some over the cassock, and over the surplice out of doors, may be defended as an attenuated form of the *cappa nigra*. But the garment that Canon 74 orders us to wear over the cassock is the far more comely parson's gown, or the university gown. For funerals, etc., the *cappa* might well be used in its original ample form.

The Amice was always worn to hang outside the other vestments, and apparelled. Apparels are so beautiful a feature in the English services that it is the more regrettable that some clergy should have discarded them, merely because they are now forbidden at Rome. The size of the amice should be from 40 in. by 32, to 44 by 36; the tapes about 75 in. long. The apparel is tacked on to the side between the tapes.

The Albe, like the amice, should always be apparelled[15]. It should be, like the surplice, much fuller than it is usually made, and the same length as the cassock. The former remarks about lace apply to every kind of vestment and ornament. Lace on albes is absolutely without authority. It is convenient for the albe to be open a little way down the front, and to be buttoned at the neck. Every server should have his own albe, which should be made to fit him.[16]

The Apparels are worn on the outside of the amice, and on the sleeves and skirt (back and front) of the albe. They may be of any colour and material that look well with the vestments, and they do not follow the seasons. For instance, red looks well with any vestments, bright blue sets off white very well, plain black serge is effective and appropriate with the red Passiontide vestments, etc. etc. Some forms of Oriental work are excellent for the purpose, and so are gold work and good old brocades: the colour should be rich and distinct; a large pattern often looks well when cut up into apparels. They can easily be made, and if tacked lightly on to the linen are not difficult to replace when this goes to the wash. A lady should be found who will be responsible for changing the apparels. Those on the sleeves should be tacked to the outside of each sleeve, a third of their length reaching over the top. Those on the skirt should rest immediately above the hem, in the middle of the front and of the back. That on the amice lies close up to the edge, at an equal distance between the tapes, and is, like the others, tacked all round.

They are simple to make. The amice-apparel should be stiffer than the others: collar-canvas is a good interlining. The albe-apparels may be interlined with linen if the material has little substance. All should be lined with white or blue linen; and an edging of cord or braid is an improvement. The dimensions vary: the following are recommended for men, but boys' apparels should be rather smaller:—Amice-apparel, 22 in. by 3½ in.; sleeve-apparels, 9 in. by from 3 to 4½; skirt do., 10 by 10 (or they may be longer and rather narrower).

The Girdle should be of linen rope. About 128 in. long is a very convenient size if it is used double, one end being then turned into a noose, and the tasselled ends slipped through.

The Stole is generally made too broad. The old ones were only about two inches across, slightly splaying at the ends. Crosses were seldom if ever put on the ends and back of the stole; but ornamentation of various kinds (sometimes the whole length of the stole) was common, as were also fringes, both on stole and maniple. The length of the eucharistic stole should be from about 8 ft. 2 in. to 9 ft: it should be long enough for the ends just to appear below the chasuble. The wretched custom of sewing a piece of lace on the middle of the stole is unnecessary, because our clergy are cleanly in their habits, they may not preach in the stole, and they cover it with the amice if they use it properly: it is a kind of anti-macassar, and belongs to that period.

The other stoles required for baptism, confession, marriage, and ministering the chalice will be little shorter, if a proper surplice is worn, and very little broader. About 99 in. is a good length. For a small church a white and a violet stole will suffice.

The Maniple, like the stole, should be narrow without crosses, and fringed. A good length is from 2 ft. 7 in. to 3 ft., and the same width and decoration as the stole. Elastic is unnecessary: if the maniple be tacked so as to leave easy room for the arm, it will keep in position of itself so long as the arms are carried properly. No button is wanted.

The Chasuble. There has been a great variety in the shape of the chasuble, not only at different periods but at one and the same time also. On the whole the tendency for the last six hundred years has been to cut down the material: this has culminated in the strange and undignified stiff little vestment now used abroad, which may fortunately be dismissed as beyond our province. But a longer and more ample form of this square chasuble was in use at the time of our Rubric. It should not be stiffened; it may have a pillar or a Latin cross, and it should be about as long as a Gothic vestment, *i.e.* about 1½ yds. from the neck behind.

But the Gothic shapes, now commonly in use amongst us, are more beautiful, and truer on the whole to our traditions. The shape most frequently seen reaches nearly to the wrists, and very good vestments can be cut on these lines. The older shape is still fuller, and the sides have to be turned back over the wrist.

A substantial silk does not need any interlining, and in any case nothing like a stiff one should be used. The best orphreys are undoubtedly the Y-shaped (except where embroidered figures under canopy work are used), but these are generally made too broad. The medieval chasuble more often had no orphreys at all. There is no need in an English vestment for the pieces of ribbon without which it seems impossible to keep a 'fiddle-back' in position. A properly made chasuble hangs straight and well of itself. A good length for a chasuble is 1½ yds. behind, and breadth at the widest part about 48 in. But they are not easy things to cut and make properly.

These vestments need not necessarily be made of silk.[17] It is a loss of effect to have the lining of the same colour as the vestment. Linings of blue linen are often very serviceable. For hot countries the lining may be dispensed with. Poor churches can make cheap and quite beautiful chasubles out of serge, unlined. As a general rule brocades or other materials bearing some design are best, with orphreys of a quite different colour and material. Embroidery is always a dangerous thing, and should only be undertaken under an artist's direction.

The Cope is nearly semi-circular in shape, about 5 ft. by 10 ft. 8 to 11; it should have an orphrey from 3 to 9 in. in width, and a hood, of which the shapes vary considerably. The vestment itself need have no stiffening, but a stout interlining of collar-canvas will be needed for the orphrey. The cope is fastened by the morse, which may be of metal or of fabric. The hood may be detachable: it may hang either from above the top of the orphrey or from below it. The hood and the bottom edge of the cope may be fringed. The cope, like the chasuble, may be of any comely material, silk or otherwise.

It may be noted that, even in the days of Puritan aggression, our Canons would not permit the ministers at cathedral churches to escape from wearing the cope. If Bishops and Deans would avoid what is acknowledged lawlessness in discarding this vestment, they would find it easier to restrain lawlessness when it appears in other directions.

The Dalmatic, for the Gospeller or Deacon, should have real sleeves, and not the mere epaulettes which have rendered the dalmatic abroad almost undistinguishable from the chasuble. The orphreys may be either two narrow strips at the sides, with apparels between, or simply one pillar.

The Tunicle, for the Epistler or Sub-deacon, only differs from the dalmatic in that it has a tendency to be somewhat less ornamental: there is no precise difference in ornament. Both may have tassels.

The tunicle for the Clerk may be somewhat simpler than that for the Epistoler. In a small church it would not matter if it were not in suite with the chasuble. In large churches the servers would probably be in accord with precedent if they too wore tunicles.

The gospeller also wears a stole over his left shoulder; both gospeller and epistler wear maniples.

The Humeral or Offertory Veil need not necessarily be in suite with the other vestments. It should be lined, and may be fringed at the ends. A good size is, either 8 ft. 7 in. by 1 ft. 8 in., or 9 to 10 ft. by 2 to 2½ ft.

The Rochet is simply a substitute for the albe. The albe needs a girdle, amice and apparels, and requires some care in the putting on. The rochet can be slipped on in a moment; and therefore it came to be very generally substituted for albes in the case of the clerks (but not of the Celebrant) at ordinary parish churches. No doubt it was for the same reason of convenience that it came to be part of the bishop's everyday dress. Lyndewode tells us that the sleeveless rochet was sometimes worn by the priest at baptisms, also for convenience.

The rochet may be described as being between the albe and the surplice. It has narrow sleeves like the albe (unless it be sleeveless, when it has a slit down each side), but only falls to within some six inches of the ground like the surplice. It should button at the neck, but it has neither amice, girdle, nor apparels.

I have stated its ancient purpose. In these days there is no less need for a garment that can be quickly slipped on. But the question will be raised, Does not the surplice suffice for this purpose? The answer is that the surplice is perfectly lawful for servers, at all rites and ceremonies, as well as for choristers: at the same time we shall be more in accordance with the Rubric if we find some use for the rochet. My own opinion is that the surplice looks best for adult servers; but that a very comely rochet can be made to suit boys. In the case of boy servers, it is of some practical importance that they should be distinguished from the choir-boys, to whom they should be models of seemly behaviour. It is here that I have found the rochet very useful as a substitute for the albe (and the servers will hardly wear albes at baptisms, children's services, and week-day Eucharists, and in many churches not at the Sunday services either). To put it in another way. When albes are worn they must be worn with apparels and apparelled amices. If the parson does not want the trouble of apparels and well-fitting albes for the servers, he should not put them into plain albes, still less into cottas, but he may very well vest them in rochets.

The Verger's Gown.—This is a very ancient garment, and the present tendency to put the Verger in parish churches into a cassock only (nearly always an ill-fitting one) is much to be regretted. The gown can be bought at any official tailor's: it is best with velvet down the front and on the collar.

Choristers' Vestments.—Where there is a surpliced choir, the men should wear, over their cassocks, surplices that are nearly or quite as full and long as those of the clergy, and the boys in proportion. The mean custom of putting them into things that are not really surplices at all is not creditable to us. The cassock, by no means always worn under the surplice, even in Rome, for long after the sixteenth century, has become a necessity since the invention of trousers. When the ceremonial ruling of the choir was used, the rulers used to wear copes at all the principal services on the principal days. They also held staves.

3. Ornaments.—The ornaments here mentioned are those which are kept in the sacristy: those which stand in the church are dealt with in other chapters. The linen should be entirely without lace, and not of a thin or flimsy description. The embroidery should be confined to the small white crosses, which serve to mark the articles for their sacred purpose.

The Corporas or Corporal is a square piece of smooth linen, not less than 20 in.: it should be of a size to lie easily on the altar; for it must not hang at all over the front. It should always be folded in the same way, the most usual being to fold it first in three parts, beginning at the front, then from the sides again in three; thus, when spread out, it is divided by the folds into 9 squares. On one of these squares, usually the front square, one small cross may be embroidered.

The Pall at the time of the Rubric was simply a second corporal. This form of pall is also best adapted to our present needs; for, after the communion, when our rubric directs that what remains of the consecrated Elements shall be covered with a fair linen cloth, the pall should be unfolded for this purpose. Thus no new-fangled 'cloth'[18] is needed for the covering of the elements. The corporal that is used as a pall may easily be differentiated from the others by having a different mark, e.g. a cross on the *outside* fold.

Sometimes a square pall, made of two or three pieces of linen stitched together, and well stiffened with starch mixed with wax, is used. In this case, the only way to cover the Elements is to place the paten on the chalice, and the pall on the paten. This is hardly a straightforward and satisfactory way of obeying our two rubrics.[19] Certainly, the use of cardboard to stiffen this sort of pall, or of blotting-paper, is absolutely wrong, nothing but linen having been allowed about the Blessed Sacrament from very ancient times. Sometimes the corporals are stiffened with starch; which is convenient, and not altogether without precedent, but the ancient canons are certainly against the use of starch.[20]

The Purificator, a napkin of soft linen or diaper, for cleansing the chalice, may be marked with a very small cross in one corner. Sometimes purificators are made so small and of such thin linen that they do not properly serve their purpose. Thirteen inches is a good size. Six purificators should be supplied with every set of altar-linen.

Thus, with a stock of two or three dozen, the clergy will not be in danger of running short and adopting the Roman custom of using the same purificators over and over again.

The Burse or Corporas Case was always used to contain the two corporals (*i.e.* corporal and pall), though chalice-veils were not. There is no rule as to its ornamentation. It should be covered with silk or other material, lined with white linen, and stiffened with cardboard. A convenient size may be from 9 to 10 in. square, the larger size being best. It should be unfastened on three sides, so that it will open like a book. Every burse should have its two corporals always kept in it.

Curiously enough, the chalice-veil, which is so common to-day, is difficult to account for under our Rubric. It is probably to be traced to the 'corporals' of silk and velvet which we find in some fifteenth and sixteenth century inventories, and may have been chalice-veils. Soto (1494-1560) notes that in very many churches, in England and elsewhere, a sort of silken cover was used for enveloping the chalice while it was on the altar except at the sacring.[21] There is no reason why the chalice-veil should be ornamented in any particular manner: the usual embroidered devices are not good. There is no need for a chalice-veil when the humeral veil is used.

Towels for drying the hands at the offertory are generally made much too small. They should be of linen diaper about 3 ft. long by 2 ft. wide; then they will rest easily on the server's arm and be convenient to use. Like purificators, they may conveniently be folded in three. While purificators and corporals are hemmed, napkins may be pulled out at the ends, or all round, in a fringe. Two to a set will suffice.

The sacred vessels should be made by some genuine craftsman who is familiar with the traditional forms.

The Chalice has varied much in size and shape: the present tendency is to make it too high: medieval examples only range from 5 to 7 inches in height. The bowl should be quite plain within and without, or it will be difficult to cleanse. An ornamental knot is usually made on the stem for convenience in holding it. On the foot a sacred device should be engraved to show the priest at which side to communicate himself and the people: the most common device was a crucifix.

The Paten is a circular plate, large enough to cover the chalice, with one or two depressions, circular or multifoil. Nearly every extant medieval example has a sacred device engraved upon it; but now that many breads are consecrated, perhaps a perfectly plain surface is more convenient.

The Ciborium is convenient for holding the breads when there are so many communicants that the paten is not safe. An extra chalice can be used for this purpose.

The ordinary Pyx is a small box (generally circular and of silver), which is kept in a purse with a cord if the Blessed Sacrament has to be carried to the sick. A bell and lantern were carried before the Blessed Sacrament on these occasions.

A private communion set is often used for the communion of the sick. One should be always kept in the sacristy. As a general rule the bowls and bases of these private chalices are made too small. In addition to the cruets there should also be a small box for the breads. The Cowley fathers have designed a convenient form of private altar for sick communions which can be bought at Mowbray's.

For poor churches it will be found that pewter is a suitable and a comely material for the sacred vessels. It is far better than shams.

The Cruets for wine and water were generally of silver or pewter; they were distinguished from each other by some mark. Glass is, however, more easy to keep clean. For glass it is better not to have metal fittings, so that if a cruet is broken it can easily be replaced; glass stoppers are the easiest to take in and out. The Whitefriars Co. make cruets.

The Bason.—Two silver basons seem to have been ordinarily used, the water being poured from one to the other. For economy, a plain glass bowl can be bought anywhere, and a little glass jug. The cruet should not be used.

A Box for Altar Breads of silver or pewter was used, and is most convenient.

The Censer needs no special description here. Where silver is out of the question, I have found that white metal is cleaner, lighter, and more effective than brass, but the metal is of course a matter of taste. The total length may be 43 in. The *incense-boat* and *spoon* are mentioned below.

The Processional Crosses may be three in number, one (which was generally of wood and painted red or green and without a figure) being reserved for Lent, and a third for funerals. Of the processional cross, as of most other things, it may be said that proportion comes first, workmanship second, and material third; the latter without the two former being worse than useless. A poor church can have a very beautiful cross of wood, which is much better than a badly designed and executed one of greater pretension. The cross should not be kept exposed out of service time. A tall locker or a stand in the vestry will be convenient, and in new churches provision should be made for this. The smallest length for cross and staff together would be about 6 ft. 8 in.

The Processional Torches, of which two will be wanted, had better be of wood (green and red were common colours). The bases should be separate and weighted with lead, so that the shafts of the torches can be easily dropped into them when they stand before the altar. If the cup of a wooden candlestick be rubbed with a little sweet oil, wax will not adhere to it. Forty-five inches is a good height.

Banners may vary considerably in size, shape, material, and device. Embroidered ones are expensive if they are worth having; and if our churches had half as many banners, and those banners had twice as much spent on them, it would be far better. At the same time, a profusion of gold and silk is nothing in itself: a banner cannot be designed by amateurs who do not understand the craft (though they can often carry out the work under advice), nor can it be ordered from a shop like a pair of boots. The common idea is that the design is nothing, and the materials everything; but the design is everything, for it includes the selection of the right materials; and the design must be paid for—and, after all, the two or three pounds thus spent is but a small proportion of the money usually wasted on pretentious and vain banners. There are good designers at the Birmingham Guild of Handicraft, and at Morris's. For an important banner it will be well to consult the Clergy and Artists' Association. I may mention as examples of what banners can be, those designed for St. Alban's, Teddington, by Mr. Skipworth, and that for Worcester Cathedral by Mr. Gere.

Of course it is true of banners as of everything else that simple ones can be made which are quite cheap and yet beautiful—if they are unpretending. The thing always is to find the right person. It is for this reason that I make no apology for recommending those societies which are artistic and not commercial in their aim, and whose business it is to find out who are those qualified to practise the arts. There are a very large number, especially among the younger artists, who understand design. The parson has no means of finding them out; and therefore he has been generally driven, in the case of embroidery, to the professional church-embroiderer, whose ignorance of the fundamentals of the art is often not less profound than his ignorance of the elements of ecclesiastical tradition.

The Wands for the Churchwardens are of wood, according to a very constant tradition in our Church, either plain, or painted white, with a few inches at the end blue or gilt. Sometimes they bear a device.

The Verge, which is carried by the officer to whom it gives his name, may be of wood tipped with metal, or of metal with a device, as in our cathedrals.

The Gospel Lectern may be of any material, and the desk may be covered with a long lectern-cloth.

The Paschal Post or Candlestick may be conveniently of painted wood.[22] It should be not less than 6 ft. high. Owing to the size of the candle it is necessary that the greater part of it should be a wooden stock, called anciently a Judas. It is better in my opinion to omit the grains of 'incense,' which are generally shams and not incense at all, and are said to be due to a mistranslation of a phrase in the *Exultet*, '*incensi hujus sacrificium*,' which really meant 'the sacrifice of this lighted candle.'

The Tenebrae Herse[23] is a triangle made generally of three pieces of wood about 3 in. broad, 1 in. thick, the lower piece 4 ft. long, the two upper pieces 3 ft. each, and fixed on to a stand similar to those used for music but more substantial; the whole may stand 5½ ft. from the ground. Along the two upper edges of the triangle should be bored 24 holes to carry the candles.[24] Both the herse and the Paschal Post should be carefully wrapt up and kept in the store-room.

There remain to be mentioned the funeral accessories.

The Bier or Herse should be higher than is generally made (say, about 4 ft.). The handles should drop slightly at the ends.

The Pall. There is at the present day an unnecessary hankering after gloom at funerals. The ancient palls mentioned in Mr. Bancroft Randall's paper on the Burial of the Dead[25] are of cloth of gold, of black velvet with wide cross all through of silver tissue, of red with a gold cross, of blue with a red cross, of black with a gold cross, and another of blue with a red cross. They were often also powdered with the badges, and had the scutcheons of the deceased sewn about the border. At the funeral of George II. a purple pall was used; the white embroidered pall used at Mr. Gladstone's funeral will also be remembered.

The Processional Cross and the Funeral Candlesticks. These may be all made of wood and painted the same colour, and that colour is not bound to be black. Mr. Randall mentions four candles to stand round the herse as a minimum. Sometimes twelve were used.

A Handbell was always rung before the funeral procession.

Other Ornaments in use at the time of the Rubric may be mentioned more summarily, as it may be questioned whether there is now a 'time of ministration' for them. For fuller information about them the reader is referred to Mr. Micklethwaite's invaluable Alcuin Tract on the *Ornaments of the Rubric*.

Although the small Lent veils may still be used, the great veil that was hung during Lent across the sanctuary is contrary to many of our rubrics and the spirit of the Prayer Book. The Monstrance and its processional Canopy raise questions which are beyond our province here. The same may perhaps be said of the Pax, holy-water vat and sprinkler, and also of the Easter Sepulchre.

The chrisom, a white garment for baptisms, was ordered by the First Prayer Book. The churching-cloth, a white veil which the woman wore, was used long after that time.

Surplices, albes, rochets, copes, chasubles, etc., as well as altar-linen, apparels, frontals, etc., are made by the *St. Dunstan Society*, which has been founded in order to make ornaments and vestments in accordance with the standard of our rubric, and under fair conditions. The price list can be obtained from the secretary, St. Dunstan Society, 7 Cambridge Terrace, Edgware Road, W.

Notes

1 See Mr. St. John Hope's collection of inventories in his paper to the St. Paul's Ecclesiological Society (vol. ii.). At Lincoln (of which we

possess the fullest inventories) there were 16 red chasubles, 3 purple, 6 green, 11 blue, 5 black, 9 white, 1 yellow, and 1 'varius.'

2 In *practice* this red would nearly always be superseded by the colour of a saint. One copy of the *Customary*, just published by Mr. Frere, seems to order *green* from the Wednesday after Trinity (26,285).

3 A perfect mine of information is provided by the paper of Mr. Hope already referred to, and by that of Dr. Legg in Vol. i. of the Transactions of the St. Paul's Ecclesiological Society

4 *E.g.* Dr. Legg says of the London Pontifical that it, 'among other improvements, allows a different and more sombre colour for the last fortnight of Lent.'

5 The mistake was caused by a rubric in the Sarum missal which directs the priest to bless the ashes in a red cope on Ash Wednesday. But this was the ferial colour; for Ash Wednesday was not then regarded as part of Lent, which began on the Sunday following, the Lent veils being hung up then.

6 This does not, of course, mean the exclusive use of so-called ecclesiastical designs.

7 See, for a careful examination of these vestments and ornaments, Mr. Micklethwaite's Alcuin Club tract on *The Ornaments of the Rubric*.

8 Rev. T. A. Lacey, in an interesting article on 'The Ecclesiastical Habit in England' (*S.P.E.S. Trans.* iv. 2) mentions a Spanish traveller during the Peninsular War who remarked with surprise that our clergy were all dressed 'like Benedictine monks.'

9 That the medieval surplice reached almost to the feet is known to every one who has seen an old brass. Since the Reformation, repeated Articles show what our 58th Canon means by a 'decent and comely surplice with sleeves.' Bp. Andrewes requires 'a comely large surplice with wide and long sleeves.' Bp. Montagu asks, 'Of what assise be the Surplices, large or scantling? For not cheapnesse but decentnesse is to be respected in the things of God.' Bp. Cosin asks, 'Have you a large and decent surplice?' And the same question we find asked at Durham since the last revision (c. 1715). See Perry, *Church Orn.*, 349, 385, 451, 461.

10 The open buttoned surplice came in about the end of the seventeenth century, owing, it is said, to the growing habit among the clergy at that time of wearing a wig. Happily the wig is now obsolete in the Church as a ceremonial head-dress; and with it the reason for an open surplice, as also for the exaggerated opening to the hood.

11 Chapter VII.

12 See Dr. W. Legg, *S.P.E.S. Trans*. iii. 'The Black Scarf and Grey Almuce,' and Fr. Robinson in iv. 3.

13 Chapter II.

14 Evidence on this and the other points here mentioned was given by me in the *Guardian* for October 13, 1897. Since then the evidence has been about doubled, and the meaning of the word 'tippet' is shown beyond dispute in Rev. Fr. Robinson's article on 'The Black Chimere,' *S.P.E.S. Trans*. iv. 3. See also Robertson *On the Liturgy*, and Perry, *Church Ornaments* (208, 216-7, 263, 294, 387, 408, 461, and xl). At Court the youngest curate is still required to wear the tippet with his cassock and gown.

15 The direction in the First Prayer Book that albes are to be 'plain,' means that they shall not be of silk or any coloured or embroidered material. It does not refer to the use of apparels, which are entirely separate vestments. E.g. Bishop Goodrich's monument in Ely Cathedral, *temp*. Elizabeth, where very gorgeous apparels are represented; and Goodrich was one of the compilers of the First Prayer Book.

16 The albe was in use as late as 1783 at Bedlow Church, Bucks (Perry, *Purchas J.*, 105).

17 In *e.g.* the inventories quoted by Blunt (lxxvii.) there are 30 vestments of cloth of gold, 6 of silver, 30 of satin, 134 of silk, 16 of sarsnet, 226 of bawdkin, 146 of damask, 54 of tissue, 9 of chamlet, 6 of fustian, 2 of buckram, 8 of dornyx, 1 of serge, and 48 various.

18 The Scotch Liturgy of 1637 directs the Elements to be covered with 'a fair linen cloth *or corporal*,' which shows that Laud and Wren knew what they were doing. The rubric was not inserted in our Book till 1662. Both Durandus and the Sarum Missal speak of the covering of the chalice with the corporal, and Durandus further shows the

identity of the pall and corporal by his use of the phrase *palla corporalis.*

19 Indeed it is a clumsy attempt to adopt the Roman pall to a purpose which is entirely different from that of the Roman rite. When the Romans do reserve the Sacrament till the end of Mass (as on Maundy Thursday), they use an additional veil for covering the same, just as we do. The 'fair linen cloth or corporal' is a necessity of our rite, because we practise reservation till the service is over (cf. J. W. Kempe, *Reservation of the Blessed Sacrament*, 25-28).

20 See Mr. Atchley on Altar Linen in the *S.P.E.S. Trans.* iv. 3.

21 Cf. Mr. Cuthbert Atchley's article on 'Variations from the Rule concerning the Materials of the Altar-linen' (*S.P.E.S. Trans.* iv. 3).

22 Craftsmen will find a description of various forms of the candlestick in Feasey's *Ancient English Holy Week Ceremonial*, cap. 9.

23 Herse or Hearse is derived from the Latin word for a harrow; it is here used in the meaning of its first derivation—'a triangular framework for holding candles' (Chambers's *Et. Dic.*). Because of the candles the word came to be applied to the bier.

24 H. J. Feasey, *Ancient English Holy Week Ceremonial*, p. 91.

25 *Transactions of the Society of St. Osmund*, vol. 1. pt. iii.

CHAPTER IV
VESTRIES

If it is difficult to put up with the single vestry of an eighteenth-century church, it is still more inconvenient to find oneself in an ordinary country church where in accordance with the ancient custom there is often no vestry at all.[1] At the present day our architects are more liberal, and I shall in this chapter assume the existence of the three vestries near the east end of the church, which are almost indispensable when there is a surpliced choir, and convenient when there is not. These will be the Priests' Vestry or Sacristy, the Choir Vestry, and the Churchwardens' Vestry. In addition to these a room where large articles can be stored will be found most useful.

The Churchwardens' Vestry, the smallest of the three, is primarily for the transaction of church business. It will promote a decorous spirit, as well as save time and money, if the little things which this room should contain are kept in a fixed place, and not in loose cardboard boxes. Besides the two or three chairs there will be a knee-hole desk, on which lies the Service Register,[2] an ink-pot of the office type, with two or three decent pens; hard by on the wall will hang the Calendar, which had best be Dr. Wickham Legg's 'Churchman's Oxford Calendar.' One of the drawers of the desk should be partitioned to contain such things as a box of nibs, pins, drawing-pins, and a rubber stamp, with a self-inking pad of the 'effective' pattern: other drawers will contain a stock of service and of notice papers, a tablet of scribbling-paper, some notepaper, envelopes, and cards for post; one or two will be reserved for the Churchwardens' books, and one or two for the special books and papers needed for the Catechism. In a safe, or at least in a locked drawer, will be kept the baptism register, marriage registers, burial register,[3] banns book, and books of certificates for marriage, banns, and baptism. In this room will be a safe in which old registers and other articles of value will be kept. On the walls may be hung a map of the parish and any portraits or other pictures of parochial interest: it is really a good work to keep in this way a memorial of the past history of the church and of the various officers who have served it. A shelf or two will be certainly useful, here as in the other rooms. A small looking-glass in each vestry will be very convenient; and, if all the vestries are carpeted or provided with matting, everybody will find it easier to be quiet.

There should be a reliable clock in some conspicuous place. A large plain round clock on the wall will be found the most useful kind.

If possible there should always be a sanitary convenience adjoining the outer vestry. In a new church this should be a properly made lavatory, with reversible basins, and every convenience of the best sanitary pattern, such as any architect can secure.

The Sacristan's cupboard had best be in the vestry nearest the church. This cupboard may have a few shelves in the upper part, and drawers of different sizes in the lower. There should be two very deep drawers, one for candle-ends, and one for dusters and polishing leathers; two long drawers for candles, of which a good stock should be laid in at a time, as wax improves by keeping. Supposing the cupboard to be a small one, 4 ft. by 5, the two bottom drawers may be 23 in. long and 9 in. deep (for dusters and candle-ends), the next two 6 in. deep and the whole length of the cupboard (for candles), the next two stages might contain six short drawers 11 in. long and 4 in. deep, and the remainder shelves, the space between the two lower shelves being divided into wide pigeon-holes by partitions.

On one of these shelves may be kept the box for the *incense*; a square tin canister, such as is often used for a tea-caddy, will do best. It should hold a pound of incense easily.

As for the incense itself, it is wisest to avoid compounds. Nothing is so good as simple *Gum Olibănum*, which is indeed 'frank' or pure incense. It can be bought at any large apothecary's for about 1s. 5d. a pound, and is cheaper as well as pleasanter and fresher than the compounds, which are for the most part rather sickly and stuffy. Sometimes two oz. of Gum Benzoin and one oz. of powdered Cascarilla bark are added; but, beyond doubling the cost, they make little difference.

The Incense Boat and Spoon should be kept in the pigeon-hole next to the Canister. If the boat is broader than the usual shape, less incense will be wasted; the lid should lift up at both ends. The spoon will be less apt to spill if it is made more like an ordinary teaspoon than is usual, and less like that used by Primitive Man.

Next to these should stand a covered earthenware jar for the charcoal. The plain brown jars that are used for cooking purposes are very suitable, and can be bought of a good shape at any china-shop. The packets of charcoal should be emptied into this, and not kept loose near the vestries, as they make dirt. If a pair of small tongs is kept near the jar, the thurifer can do his work without soiling his hands. The charcoal can be heated in a minute if the lumps are put into a wire spoon with a wooden handle, and held over the gas. As little charcoal should be used as possible; for charcoal fumes are not pleasant.

A good plan, when there is room, is for the thurifer to have a narrow cupboard of his own in which to keep these articles. In this case the cupboard should be divided by a partition from the top to within twelve inches of the bottom. One side will be for the censer, which will hang free from a long peg; the wire spoon and tongs can hang near it on small pegs. The other side will be divided horizontally into shelves for the boat, canister and jar. At the bottom of the cupboard will be a deep drawer, in which extra packets of charcoal may be stored; for charcoal is cheaper if bought in large quantities. If there is no cupboard for the censer it can be hung on an iron bracket about six inches long, with a crook at the end. Or it may hang from a hook on a small shelf, on which the canister and charcoal-jar can stand. This is the simplest arrangement. But in any case the censer should hang quite free, touching neither the wall nor the ground.

The Choir Vestry should be as large as possible, and very long for its breadth; so that the choir can form up in a double row. A card with the word 'Silence' may advantageously be hung on the wall. Large shallow cupboards will take up most of the walls; these will contain separate pegs for each cassock and for each surplice, each pair of pegs bearing the owner's name and number. If there is not a shelf over the pegs on which hats can be placed, another row of larger pegs must be provided elsewhere for this purpose. Every cassock and surplice should be numbered; and a lady should be found who will take charge of all the surplices, send them to the wash, and keep them in repair.

An inventory of every bit of linen belonging to the church should be carefully made, and kept up to date.

The Sacristy. When many vestments are kept, a *Press* will be wanted; though some small churches may find two or three wooden yokes, hanging in a cupboard, sufficient. They hold chasubles and copes very well, and can be bought through a tailor or an ironmonger for a few pence.

The number of presses will depend upon the size of the Sacristy and the number of services. In churches where there is a high Celebration every Sunday, it is convenient to keep the vestments for this service in one large press, 9 feet long or more (to enable the three ministers to vest at it), but divided by a partition into two sets of drawers. A smaller press can then be reserved for low Celebrations, for which separate chasubles, etc., will be needed.

An ordinary press maybe 3½ ft. high, 4 ft. 9 in. long, and 2 ft. 9 in. broad. The drawers should be shallow (2 in. inside), so that only one set of vestments may be kept in each: this saves time and spares the vestments. If, in ordering a press, the parson has twice as many drawers made as he seems to want, he will be glad of the provision before very long. The veils and burses should be kept with the vestments of their colour. The top drawer will be found useful for apparelled amices; and, if there is no cupboard for the priests' albes, they can be folded in the bottom drawer if it is made, say, 6 in. deep. A cupboard for the priests' albes and girdles is a convenience, but in towns it must be as nearly air-tight as possible. A cedar-wood lining to the drawers keeps away the moth, and a lining of cloth dyed in saffron preserves gold embroidery. A piece of white cloth or stout linen laid over the vestments in each drawer will help to keep the dirt from them. Heavily embroidered vestments will need cotton-wool under the folds when they are put away. Sometimes presses have a folding lid on the top to keep the vestments clean when they are laid out. A cheaper plan is to cover them with a piece of white cloth. The top of the press where the vestments are laid out should have a piece of white cloth or linen fixed on it with drawing-pins. The vestments should be laid out in the following order:—chasuble, stole, maniple, girdle, albe, and on the top of all the amice. If there is a procession, the cope will be laid above the chasuble, unless there is a cope-stand.

A Cope-stand is extremely useful. It consists of a wooden upright, about 5½ feet high, resting on a firm base, and having a well-rounded yoke on the top. After the procession the cope is slipped on to the stand in a moment, and the morse fastened. It can then be folded up at leisure after the service. If there is a large air-tight cupboard copes can always be kept thus on their stands with a linen cloth over them.

A crucifix should hang above the press. Under it may be placed the hymn, *Come Holy Ghost* and the 43rd Psalm *Judica me*, which were formerly appointed to be said while vesting.

A basin, if possible fitted with a tap and drain, should be provided for the parson to wash his hands therein before celebrating. Near it will hang a jack-towel.

A little square basin, hanging on a bracket under a filter, should also be provided for the purificators. After each service the purificator can be rinsed in this basin, and then put by for the wash in a special basket or on a rail. The basin should be emptied in the piscina. The filter will also supply the pure water for the Eucharist.

A Safe for the vessels is almost a necessity. When there is none, a niche for the chalice and paten must be made in the hanging Altar-cupboard. This small cupboard should be fixed to the wall at a convenient height, and near it may be a bracket where the vessels under their veil can be placed before service. There should be at least two shallow drawers in the cupboard, and two shelves, one divided by partitions. In one drawer will be kept the clean purificators and napkins, in another the spare corporals. Lavender in these drawers is not only pleasant but serves also to keep away insects. In the niches of the partitioned shelf will be kept the cruets, the two boxes for the breads, the small ewer and basin, the shell for baptism, if one is used; the top shelf might be tall enough to contain the spare bottles of wine. It may be divided into three niches, one large for the stock of wine, one narrow for the altar-books, one large enough to take the chalice and paten. An extra shelf and drawer will generally come in useful: stoles may be kept in the drawer.

Near this small cupboard may stand a larger one for altar-linen. An ordinary bedroom shape may serve; but it will be better if it is made with shallower drawers. The two top short drawers of the bedroom type will be useful for storing such things as frontal apparels and Lenten veils; but, as they will in that case be seldom used, they may be more advantageously at the bottom. One drawer will be needed for the spare linen cloths of the high altar (one fair linen and two undercloths will suffice); another drawer for the linen belonging to other altars; another will be found useful for keeping the sets of vestment apparels that are not in actual use. If there is no chest for the frontals, and if they can be folded, space may be found for them here.

The Frontal Chest will stand in some convenient spot near the altar. If the frontals are stretched on frames, the chest should open at the top and be large enough for twice as many frontals as are in use. A chest that is only large enough for the colours in use, will prove a nuisance when somebody presents a new frontal.

If the frontals are not stretched, a cupboard should be provided with shallow shelves large enough for each frontal to be folded in four, with a shelf for frontlets, and some spare shelves.

A special Cupboard should be reserved for the servers' albes, etc., their cassocks and shoes being kept elsewhere. Two pegs at least will be needed for each server, one for his albe and girdle, and one for his surplice or rochet: a shelf above can be kept for the apparelled amices. If a succession of boys serve at the week-day services a surplice or rochet had better be hung for them somewhere else. Washing is a very expensive item, and if the servers' cupboard is kept locked from Sunday to Sunday, and is nearly air-tight, the albes, etc., will keep clean twice as long as they otherwise would.

Yet another cupboard will be that for Music, which should be divided into large pigeon-holes. If each set of music is kept strictly in its place by the Librarian (who must be a responsible person), and duly inventoried, tidiness will be gained and much money saved. Each set of music should be kept in a brown-paper bag, or, in the case of special services seldom used, in a cardboard box. Special hymns, carols, etc., for congregational use, should be carefully stored in the upper shelves. Everything in the music-cupboard should be clearly labelled.

It is obvious that many churches have not room for all the cupboards which I have described. In this case, composite cupboards will have to be made. But, in any case, care should be taken that there is really a place for everything, even if cupboards and chests have to be put up in the church itself (which was the usual ancient practice). Wherever a cupboard is, it should be painted a pleasant colour, or stained green. Varnished pitch-pine, and imitation-wood stains, are almost as destructive of warmth and beauty as is oak-graining. The usual practice is to make cupboards somewhat at random when other places overflow; but, if the parson will consider, before he calls in the carpenter, exactly what the requirements of the church are likely to be, I do not think he will regret a consideration of the hints I have given.

The Duties of the Sacristan. The best proverb for the parson is, that if you want a thing well done you must get other people to do it. He had much better not spend his time fussing about the accessories of divine service, nor will he find one helper sufficient. The whole responsibility should be laid upon the Sacristan, who had much better be a layman. The sacristan's position is a most important one, and he must be devout, sensible, and even-tempered. Generally it will be found that he also makes the best Clerk. He need not do a very great deal himself, but he must see that everything is done, which means that he must be kind and pleasant in manner as well as careful.

He will see that a list of servers is posted on the wall for every service in the week; and when any one is to be away he will fill his place. He will see that everything is ready five minutes before service begins on Sunday—the vestments laid out, the candles lit by the torchbearer, and the charcoal heated by the thurifer. He will gently superintend the band of helpers, who are needed if everything is to be kept as the things pertaining to God's worship ought to be kept. For nearly all these duties I have found women to be best, only they need to have their realms well defined and protected, and unless they are responsible to the sacristan there will sometimes be trouble. One lady should be found to put out the vestments every day. Her work will require much neatness of method. She may also be responsible for washing and mending the albes, etc., of clergy and servers. Another will be needed to polish the brass work and to trim the candles, which require two or three visits a week (a lad may clean the brass, but women are more reliable). Another to dust the high-altar and see to the altar-cloths, another to see to the chapel. Often another lady may be found, who has not much time to be in and out of the church, but can undertake the useful task of washing the purificators. The Verger is generally the best person to change the frontals. If there are several helpers, each responsible for his or her own piece of work, and all responsible to the Sacristan, and through him to the Parson, the most perfect cleanliness and order can be secured, a good deal of money will be saved, and those who work for the church will love it better and use it more.

It is impossible to lay down rules for washing, etc., but the following hints may be found useful:—

Times.—Wash the fair linen cloth of the altar once a month, the undercloths once a quarter.

Strip the altar entirely twice a year on a fine day, from morning till evening, so that everything may be well aired; and thoroughly clean everything connected with it.

Wash the corporals once a month. (This will not always apply to those in the green and violet burses.) The towels once a week.

Let a responsible person, wash the purificators every Saturday.

Let all the linen be clean on the greater festivals.

Wash the chalice and paten once a week with soap and water.

Rinse the cruets every day, and wash them thoroughly once a week. Clean brass every week.

The Verger will generally be responsible for dusting the church; seeing that the font, pulpit, lamps (which need hot water), etc., are clean.

Methods.—Wash the linen in warm water, with white soap. To take out ink-spots, dip the part into melted tallow before washing. To take out wine-stains, hold the part in boiling milk.

To remove wax from stuffs, cover with a piece of blotting-paper and iron with a hot iron. To remove grease, clean with a flannel moistened with turpentine. Wax can easily be removed from the tops of candlesticks if they have been rubbed with a little oil.

To clean brass, rub with polishing paste, and polish afterwards with a leather. A drop of oil of vitriol in the paste will remove tarnish. It is much less trouble if it be kept clean every week.

Lacquered brass never looks nearly so well as polished brass. It is best, if any one can be found to see to the polishing, to remove lacquer, which may be done with oxalic acid.

To clean silver, use whiting, polishing afterwards with wash-leather. Sweet oil removes burnt incense from silver thuribles.

Painted wood-work, especially if it be covered with a coat of varnish, can be easily cleaned with soap and water.

Stone should be cleaned with brush, soap and water, but never hearthstoned.

To clean wax candles, wipe them with a cloth damped with spirits of wine or turpentine.

Stains may be removed from printed books by a solution of citric acid. Old altar-linen should be burnt.

Notes

1 The practice in the average parish church of the middle ages was to keep the vestments in chests about the church. They were put on the altar before service, and the priest vested at the altar. This might still be done in some very small churches: but our modern habits are against it.

2 Canon 52 orders the names of all strange preachers to be entered in a book kept for that purpose.

3 Canon 70 orders a parchment book for christenings, weddings, and burials to be kept in a 'sure coffer' with three locks and keys.

CHAPTER V
MATTINS, EVENSONG, AND LITANY

Some General Customs may first be noticed. Bowing towards the altar never quite died out in England.[1] It is thus commended by Canon 7 of 1640: 'We therefore [*i.e.* on account of the "pious," "profitable," and "edifying" nature of outward acts] think it very meet and behoveful, and heartily commend it to all good and well-affected people, members of this Church, that they be ready to tender unto the Lord the said acknowledgment, by doing reverence and obeisance both at their coming in and going out of the said churches, chancels or chapels, according to the most ancient custom of the Primitive Church in the purest times, and of the Church also for many years of the reign of Queen Elizabeth.'

With regard to bowing at the Holy Name, Canon 18 of 1603 orders: 'When in time of Divine service the Lord Jesus shall be mentioned, due and lowly reverence shall be done by all persons present, as it hath been accustomed.' This was revived again by Convocation in 1662.

The ancient custom of turning to the east at the Creeds and *Glorias*, was also long maintained.[2] In 1686 Archdeacon Hewetson wrote to the great Bishop Wilson (then only at his ordination as deacon) that he should 'turn towards the east whenever the *Gloria Patri* and the creeds are rehearsing.' Of this and other customs he says, 'which thousands of good people of our Church practise at this day.'[3] The fact that Roman Catholics do not now turn to the east at the *Gloria* and Creed is no reason for our omitting to do so. An old English Canon also enjoins the practice of bowing at the *Gloria*.[4]

The Sign of the Cross used publicly to be made at the *Gloria Tibi*, at the end of *Gloria in Excelsis*, and at the *Benedictus* in the Mass. Canon 30, to which we are specially referred by the rubric at the end of the baptismal service, clearly defends the Sign of the Cross, not only for baptism, but as in itself a good and primitive custom:—'The honour and dignity of the name of the Cross begat a reverent estimation even in the Apostles' times of the sign of the Cross, which the Christians shortly after used in all their actions.'[5]

Some people have lately introduced the practice of priest and people saying both clauses of the *Gloria Patri* together. This must be due to ignorance, for the practice is not even Roman. Our own rubric orders quite clearly that 'at the end of every Psalm throughout the year' the *Gloria* shall be said as a versicle and response; for it puts the word *'Answer'* before the second clause 'As it was in the beginning.' etc. When the psalms are sung, the *Gloria* should be sung in the same way and not full. When the psalms are said, the *Gloria* should be said also.

After a long struggle, the Church of England succeeded in putting an end to the custom of sitting at the psalms.[6] The practice of Roman Catholics is hardly a sufficient justification for the parson to revert to the old Puritan habit, unless he is too tired to render the accustomed homage; in which case he is still ordered by the rubric, inserted at the last revision, to stand for the *Gloria Patri*. The alternate reading of the Psalms likewise rests upon tradition, and was equally opposed by the Puritans, who preferred the more sacerdotal practice of the minister saying all the verses himself.

The wretched custom of making one morning service out of two and a half is now happily dying out; and, with it, the more terrible practice of introducing a pause in the middle of the Communion Service, in order that the bulk of the congregation may absent themselves from the Holy Mysteries. Neither practice is in any way provided for in our Prayer Book. The three services are distinct, and there is no mention of any pause in the Communion Service during which the people may go away, and no provision whatever for giving the blessing in the middle of the service. I suppose nothing has so much caused the young (and not the young only) to dislike going to church as the first practice, and nothing has so much discouraged Communion as the second.

The practice grew up gradually. Heylyn[7] writes (1638):— 'This was the ancient practice of the Church of England … mattins to begin between six and seven; the second or communion service not till nine or ten; which distribution still continues in the cathedral church of Winchester, in that of Southwell, and some others,' the Puritans at that time wishing the services joined. John Johnson[8] in 1709 speaks of the making one service of Mattins, Litany, and Ante-Communion as an innovation.

At the same time it is liturgically correct to make the Litany a prelude to the Holy Eucharist. The Injunctions of 1547 order that the Litany shall be said 'immediately before high mass.' Heylyn[9] tells us that in his time 'in some churches, while the Litany is saying, there is a bell tolled, to give notice unto the people that the communion service is now coming on.' This seems a practice that falls in well with our conditions to-day, when the Litany is said, and not sung.

Mattins should come first, and the Litany is ordered in the rubric 'to be said or sung after Morning Prayer,' which does not necessarily mean immediately after.

The needs of parishes will differ much, but certain suggestions may be made:—(1) The Eucharist, as the greatest service of Christendom, will be given the place of honour; that is to say it will be fixed at the time when people can best attend: this under our present conditions would naturally be the case if the rubric were obeyed which orders the sermon to be preached after the Creed at the Holy Communion. (2) If there be music only at one service, that service will be the Eucharist. (3) Long services drive the people away whom Christ sets us to win, therefore the divisions must be kept, and the bell rung either before each service, or during the Litany. If the Eucharist is at the usual church hour (say at eleven), then Mattins and Litany come before it; and many will be glad to be present,[10] but those who feel the strain of many services can easily come in during the ringing. I fancy that many people feel the Litany intolerably long if it is sung kneeling, but appreciate it and really follow it if it is said.

Lights. There has been a good deal of unnecessary confusion on the subject of altar-lights. The universal pre-Reformation custom is at one with post-Reformation English custom in using two lights on the altar, and no more.

The only distinction is that, in post-Reformation England, churches very often fell below the ideal,[11] owing to Puritan influences; while before the Reformation one candle only was generally regarded as sufficient, and the candlesticks were portable, and generally removed out of service-time. The ancient use of two candles survived even in the Roman Church, in many places, well into the middle of the eighteenth century, only gradually succumbing to the debased taste of that period.

So far it must have been clear to all that our Ornaments Rubric gives no sanction whatever to a departure from the unbroken English custom of setting two lights only on the altar. But certain people, reading carelessly, or by second-hand, the directions of the Sarum Consuetudinary, have imagined that it is therein ordered to put six lights on the altar, and two on the steps at certain high festivals. This is not the case. Two only were placed on the altar, even on the greatest feasts: the rest were placed elsewhere, two were in the standards, and on principal and greater doubles, 'the remaining four,' says Mr. Isherwood[12] in his learned paper on the subject,' may terminate the four poles which support the curtain rods of the altar.' Lights were also placed on the rood-beam and other places not connected with the altar.

But—and it is a very large but—even this modest use of lights was only the local custom in a great cathedral. Ordinary parish churches did not have so many, and local custom differed, the one feature in common being that never more than two stood on the altar. We are not in the least bound to follow the peculiar customs of Salisbury Cathedral, beautiful and instructive as they are. Some large churches may do so; but most will do better to be content with two lights for unsung Eucharists, and for sung Mattins and Evensong on ordinary Sundays; and with four lights for the sung Eucharist always, and for Mattins and Evensong on Holy-days. Others may on the great festivals care to have a light also at the end of each curtain rod.[13]

Such childish things as branch candlesticks and other small candlesticks need only be mentioned to be condemned. They are used abroad for the very different purpose of Benediction, and have no meaning on our altars. They offend both against good taste and ecclesiastical propriety; luckily they are not lawful in our Church, for the Ornaments Rubric knows them not.

Mattins and Evensong are ordered by the Prayer Book to be said every day by all priests and deacons. The parish-priest is also ordered to 'say the same in every church or chapel where he ministereth,' having a bell tolled beforehand, if he be at home and be not otherwise reasonably hindered. Indeed, the continuous reading of the psalms and lessons is given in the earliest preface to the Prayer Book, 'Concerning the Service of the Church,' as the reason why an English Prayer Book was written—why, in fact, there was any Reformation at all. The daily recitation of these offices is, therefore, one of the things which the parish-clergy are paid to do, and they are bound as a matter of common honesty to do so.[14] Nor can any act of Parliament free them from the obligation to say the service without mutilation. The authority for any modification of a service rests with the Ordinary. The clergy should find out what hours are most convenient for the people, and most likely to secure a good attendance. When it is known beforehand that an office cannot be said on a certain day, notice should be given on the Sunday before.

It is usual to say the beautiful Prayer for All Conditions and General Thanksgiving, both in Mattins and Evensong. Excellent as the practice is in most places, it is necessary to point out exactly what the rubrics order in the matter. The rubrics both at Mattins and Evensong lay special stress on the *daily* use of the *first three collects*; but the rubrics after the Anthem at Mattins and Evensong say nothing about the Prayers and Thanksgivings; that at Mattins only orders the use of the prayers for Queen, Royal Family, and Clergy and People when the Litany is not read; that at Evensong gives no order as to the use even of these prayers, but presumably intends them to be used, at least when there is an Anthem (see below).

The rubric before the Prayer for All Conditions appoints it 'to be used at such times when the Litany is not appointed to be said.' Gunning, who wrote the prayer, would not allow it to be used at Evensong, when he was Master of St. John's College, Cambridge, declaring that he had composed it only for morning use as a substitute for the Litany.[15] Its place, also, among the 'Prayers and Thanksgivings upon Several Occasions' is also against its constant use. The General Thanksgiving has no order as to when it is to be used. That for Parliament is 'to be read during their Session.'

Therefore, although the minister may have the right to use what extra prayers he considers advisable, the general custom goes beyond what is ordered in the Prayer Book. In certain places, and on certain occasions, as when there is a baptism during the service, it may certainly be shortened by these omissions.

It has, furthermore, been urged by some that even the five prayers printed in the Morning and Evening offices are not intended to be used at unsung services. The contention is that the rubrics after the Third Collect— 'Here followeth the Anthem,' and 'Then these five prayers'—are to be read together, and thus mean that the five prayers are only to be used when there is an anthem. 'In Quires and Places where they sing, here followeth the Anthem. Then these five prayers following are to be read here,' etc. This curtailment of the service is in accordance with the ancient models, and with the Mattins and Evensong of the First Prayer Book, which also omitted the Introduction to the office up to the *Paternoster*. The peculiar mutilations of the Shortened Services Act are, on the contrary, both liturgically incorrect, and against the plain intention of the preface Concerning the Service of the Church, which, as I have already said, bases the Reformation itself mainly upon the mutilations of the Psalms and Lessons which had crept into the Church.

MATTINS.

Mattins may be said on Sundays, but it is better that it should be sung. It may also be solemn; in which case the same ceremonies will be observed as at solemn Evensong, the altar being censed at the *Benedictus*. The *Venite* may only be omitted on Easter Day and on the nineteenth day of the month. The *Jubilate* may only be substituted for the *Benedictus* when that hymn is read in the lesson for the day and on St. John Baptist's day. A general and appropriate custom is to substitute the *Benedicite*[16] for the festal *Te Deum* during Advent, and from Septuagesima till Easter.

At sung Mattins the candles should be lit, for preference the standards, except on festivals when four are lit. Anciently each clerk went to his place in the choir separately, and then said his prayer privately. At the present day it is more usual for the choir to enter in order, after a prayer in the vestry, but there is no reason why this prayer should be intoned.

The musical part of the service should not begin till the priest says 'O Lord, open thou our lips,' and the people's mouths are opened for praise. The service should then be sung until the end of the third collect, after which the remaining prayers may be said without note. It is far more seemly and impressive, if, following the ancient custom, the General Confession be said in a humble voice, just loud enough to be heard (*privatim ut audiatur*), and also the Lord's Prayer.[17] The opening Sentence[18] should be said in a 'loud voice,' as a signal that the service has commenced, and it may be monotoned; but the Exhortation and Absolution should be said in the natural voice. If this plan were more generally adopted, the popular dislike, very common among the working classes, to intoned services, would tend to disappear. Choir services were never meant to be intoned throughout, but to vary from the solemn quietness of the penitential introduction, to the joyful song of the central part, and back to the quiet intercessory prayers of the close.

The priest should always turn to the people when he says the Exhortation, and also for the whole of the Absolution, and when he says 'Praise ye the Lord,' and 'The Lord be with you.' The rubric about the lessons is clear that the reader shall 'so stand and turn himself as he may best be heard of all such as are present'; the lessons therefore should be read as audibly and as naturally as possible, 'distinctly with an audible voice.' The rubric implies that the *prayers* need not be said in the best accoustic position; but anything like 'clipping or mangling' them is forbidden not only by our own but by every other Church, the Roman Church itself having made frequent pronouncements against it. At the same time, drawling or mouthing the service is equally to be avoided.

The lessons may be read by a layman. Up to 1662 the rubric had 'the minister that readeth,' and often that minister was a layman (the clerk reading at least the first lesson). In 1662 the rubric was altered to 'he that readeth,' which puts the matter beyond dispute. The reader must begin and end the lessons according to the rubric— 'Here beginneth,' etc.

All should turn to the east for the *Glorias* and Creed. It is an old English custom to bow at the *Holy, Holy, Holy,* in the *Te Deum,* but not at the mention of the word in the *Magnificat.*

The Versicles are a preparation for the Collects which follow. Hence the priest should stand for the Collects as well. The words 'all kneeling' need no more apply to the priest than does the order 'all meekly kneeling' at the communion of the people. The matter is made quite clear by the Prayer Book of 1549, which has the direction, 'the Priest standing up.' A deacon will of course omit the Absolution at the beginning of the office.

The Anthem of the rubric (originally 'Antiphon,' old English, *antesn,* *i.e.* a hymn sung in alternate parts) has a wide meaning: hymns may be in prose as well as in verse, e.g. the *Te Deum* is a hymn; on the other hand the Book of 1549 called the *'Turn thou us'* of the Commination Service an anthem. Custom sanctions a metrical hymn (though such hymns are nowhere ordered except in the Ordination Service) at this point; and if the Office Hymn has not been sung before the *Benedictus,* or at evensong before *Magnificat* (which was the old liturgical place), it may be sung now.

When anthems are sung it is better not to stand for them. They are, like the sermon, given for the edification of the people. The people should therefore adopt the position best suited for hearing them. No outward action of the body should be without meaning, if it is to be 'pious in itself, profitable to us, and edifying to others.' Standing has always been a solemn act of reverence in church, almost as solemn as kneeling, and there can be no place less appropriate for such an act, and no place where its adoption is more likely to destroy its meaning, than the singing of the anthem, even in these music-worshipping days.

When the Litany is read, only the Prayer of St. Chrysostom and the Grace must be said after the Third Collect.

The General Thanksgiving should be said by the priest alone, as the *Amen* is printed in italics.

When there are any specially to be prayed for, or any who desire to return thanks, the custom is for the minister to stand up, before commencing the Prayer for All Conditions or the General Thanksgiving, and to announce it. He then uses in the prayer the sentence in parentheses.

SOLEMN EVENSONG.

For convenience, I shall treat here of Solemn Evensong, since for the plain service the directions as to Mattins will suffice. As for the Canticles, *Magnificat* and *Nunc Dimittis* should always be sung; they are (with *Benedictus*) the Evangelical Canticles, and have from time immemorial formed part of the daily offices of the Church; it will be noticed that the rubrics do not order them to be replaced by the alternative psalms when they occur also in the lessons for the day.

The candles will be lit; if two only, then the standards are to be preferred. In the vestry the two torchbearers will be ready with their torches lighted. The socket-bases of the torches must not be on the altar-step, but by the sedilia on each side of the priest's faldstool. The servers will all be vested in cassock and long surplice. It has not yet been proved that they may wear albes and amices for Evensong. If they do, it may be found convenient to reserve this distinction for festivals. Black cassocks look far better than red ones, which play havoc with the general effect of colour, and besides cannot be worn with albes. Dr. W. Legg denies that red cassocks are sanctioned by English tradition at all, and so experienced an ecclesiastic as Cardinal Manning spoke gravely of their bad moral effect.

The officiant will wear over his surplice a cope of the colour of the day, unless the church possess only one or two copes. The other clergy will wear, over their surplices, tippets (*i.e.* scarves) and the hoods of their degree. The officiant may also wear tippet and hood under his cope, but never a stole.

The choir in their surplices and cassocks may proceed first into the chancel with the other clergy. When they are in their places, the officiant, preceded by the torchbearers, will enter. They kneel together before the altar; they then rise and walk to the sedilia,[19] the first torchbearer before and the second behind the officiant. Arrived at the sedilia, they remain standing while one of the other clergy from his stall takes the first part of the service to the end of the Lord's Prayer. The officiant takes up the service at 'O Lord open thou our lips,' which he sings. The first torchbearer will have all the necessary music, etc., on the credence or other convenient place, and will see that he always gives the chant-book or prayer-book opened at the right page. Where there is room the priest should have a small fald-stool to kneel on.

As soon as the *Magnificat* has been precented, the officiant, with the torchbearers, one before and one behind him, proceeds to the front of the altar. At the same time, the thurifer and boat-bearer enter with the censer and boat: they go to the right of the priest, as he stands on the pavement; the thurifer opens the censer, and holds it up, while the priest takes incense from the boat. Having blessed the incense, he takes the censer, and goes up to the altar, which he censes in the usual way, the torch-bearers standing by their candles, and the thurifer going round to be ready for the censer at the south end of the foot-pace. Having given the censer up, the priest comes down in the middle to his former place on the pavement; he then returns to the sedilia, accompanied by the torchbearers as before. The thurifer, after censing the priest with three double swings, may proceed to the censing of officials in the usual way.

The priest and torchbearers sit for the lesson, stand for the *Nunc Dimittis* and Creed, and kneel as the rubric directs at '*Let us pray.*' At the last Response to the Versicles the priest and torchbearers go to the centre of the pavement as before the censing. The torchbearers stand facing one another on either side of the priest, holding their torches so as to shed the best light on the book, till the end of the Collects. They then go to the vestry by the shortest way. The priest, having taken off the cope, returns, still wearing tippet, hood, and surplice, to his own stall; the servers sit in convenient places in the choir.[20] The rest of the service is said in choir in the usual manner.

Generally the alms are collected during the hymn after the Sermon, and the service concludes with a blessing. There is no authority for the presentation of the alms at the Holy Table at choir services, and it certainly seems more correct for the server to take them straight to the credence or vestry, and for the service to be ended from the pulpit. But if this is not done, then the following is the best method:—The server appointed for the purpose will watch for the churchwardens; and, as soon as they leave the west end of the church and proceed with their basons up the middle alley, he will fetch the large bason or alms-dish; as he does so, the priest will leave his stall and proceed up to the foot-pace, standing before the altar, and never looking round. Meanwhile the server will go down the chancel-steps, and receive the alms in his bason (which he has carried up to this point in a perpendicular position). He will then go straight up to the altar, and stand at the right of the priest (not behind him, as in that case the priest will be apt to look nervously round). The priest will then turn towards him, take the bason, and offer it by slightly raising it,[21] saying, perhaps, as he does so, a private prayer. He places it on the altar, whence the server takes it to the credence. A server will fetch away the bason after service: it does not look well for the priest to carry out the bason at the conclusion of the service as if it were his own private booty.

When the hymn is over, the priest may turn to the people, saying *'The Lord be with you'*; they reply *'And with thy spirit,'* and turning to the holy Table he says *'Let us pray.'* This gives the people time to settle down quietly on their knees, and avoids the unseemly clatter which happens when there is no introduction. The priest, standing, may then say some collect appropriate to the occasion (e.g. to the season or the sermon); he then turns and pronounces a blessing. It is not appropriate to use the Mass-blessing (or half of it) at Mattins or Evensong; it always occurs in the Prayer Book in connection with Communion. The Prayer Book does indeed give a form of blessing for the bishop at the end of the Confirmation service like the second half of the Mass-blessing, but with a difference in the last words— *'be upon you, and remain with you for ever.'* At the end of the Commination service it gives another— *'The Lord bless us, and keep us; the Lord lift up the light of his countenance upon us, and give us peace, now and for evermore,'* which might, with the permission of the Ordinary, be put into the second person. It hardly seems suitable to use the beautiful Commendation in the office for the Visitation of the Sick (*'Unto God's gracious mercy,'* etc.) for ordinary public occasions. Another simple and suitable blessing is, *'God the Father, God the Son, and God the Holy Ghost bless, preserve and keep you this night and for evermore.'* As there is no authority for any blessing at all at the conclusion of Evensong, permission ought to be sought in any case.

If Evensong be solemn every Sunday, it will be convenient to mark the red-letter days by a Procession, as follows:—

During the hymn after the sermon (after he has presented the alms[22]), the officiant will go into the vestry and put on his cope;

the torchbearers will light their torches; the thurifer will see that the charcoal is alight; the clerk or cross-bearer will have ready the processional cross. Proceeding with the servers to the choir by the short way, the priest stands in the midst facing east with the thurifer and boat-bearer behind him, the cross-bearer behind the thurifer, the verger with his gown and wand behind the cross-bearer; if it be the custom of the church to carry banners, the bearers will be stationed in a convenient place at the side with their banners.

Turning to the thurifer the priest puts incense into the censer in the usual manner, and blesses it; meanwhile the music may commence.[23] When the incense has been blessed, the cross-bearer and the other servers turn and follow the verger, who leads the procession at once. A good custom is for the churchwardens to wait at the chancel-gates, and drop into the procession behind the verger. It passes round the south side of the church, in the following order:—Verger, Churchwardens, Cross, Thurifer and Boat-bearer, the two Torchbearers abreast, Officiant in cope, Choir-boys, Choir-men, other clergy in tippet and hood.

A station should be made before the Rood, all standing still while the priest says (without turning) a versicle, and after the response a suitable collect. The hymn may then be proceeded with.

At the end of the procession, the verger goes to the sanctuary-steps, when he turns and stands at one side; the thurifer and boat-bearer go to the opposite side, the cross-bearer turns to allow the priest to pass him, and then faces east behind him, and the torch-bearers stand facing east at their usual places, the priest between them. The choir may stand in their stalls or in the chancel. After the Versicles, Collect, and Blessing, the priest and servers go out the short way, followed by the choir and other clergy.

THE LITANY.

The Litany is to be said on Wednesdays and Fridays as well as Sundays. No direction is given in our book as to where or how the Litany is to be 'sung or said'; but, from the 1st year of Edward VI. to the time of Cosin it was several times appointed to be said in a special place in the midst of the church, and a faldstool is mentioned. A rubric in our Commination Service also speaks of 'the place in which they are accustomed to say the Litany,' and implies that the 'clerks' (in this sense the readers of the responses) knelt with the 'priests' at the same place. The choir may therefore kneel in the middle alley around and in front of the faldstool, or, what is occasionally more convenient, the faldstool may stand in the choir itself, as was sometimes the custom (Robertson, p. 135; illust. in Chambers, p. 129), and is still in many cathedrals, and at Ordination services: this latter position in *medio chori* is the ancient one.

If the Litany is sung in procession[24] (which is not forbidden in our book, and was the old custom) stations should be made, somewhat as follows:—All standing before the altar, the first *Kyries* are said. At *'Remember not,'* all turn, and the procession starts (verger, cross, torches, incense, etc., in the usual order), singing the Deprecations, Obsecrations, and Petitions as it goes. In most churches a long procession will be needed, first down the south alley, then up the midst, down the north alley, and up the midst again for the station.[25] The procession should go very slowly, and be timed to reach the chancel-screen at the end of the last Petition. At *'Son of God,'* a station is made before the Rood at the chancel-screen, all the choir standing till the end of the prayer. At the first antiphon, *'O Lord arise,'* the priest goes slowly up to the sanctuary, where all form up in time for the *Gloria*, and the Litany is finished, all standing before the altar.

Care must be taken by the verger, who times the procession, that it shall arrive before the Rood at the right time; if the petitions are not finished he must walk very slowly at the end.

Notes

1 The Canons at Oxford Cathedral have always done so on going out of the choir. In Cookson's *Companion to the Altar* (1784, published with his *Family Prayer Book* and dedicated to the Bishop of Winchester) the communicant is told 'rise from your knees, bow towards the altar, and retire to thy seat' (p. 31).

2 At Manchester Cathedral, according to Blunt(7), it was 'still maintained' in 1866.

3 Keble, *Life of Wilson*, i. 22. Among the customs practised by 'thousands of good people,' in 1686, are: 'nor ever to turn his back upon the altar in service-time,' 'to bow reverently at the name of

Jesus,' and 'to make obeisance at coming into, or going out of, the church, and at coming up to and going down from the altar.' There was quite a literature upon the subject in the early part of the eighteenth century, and the usage was generally maintained.

4 Of 1351.—Wilkins, *Conc.* iii. 20.

5 See *e.g.* Tertullian, *de Corona Militis*, iii. 4.

6 Abbey and Overton, ii. 472-3. In the seventeenth century sitting for the Psalms was universal, and Laud was charged with innovation for standing at the *Gloria*, for which there was then no rubric, Robertson, ix.

7 *Antidotum*, iii. 61, Cf. Robertson, 112.

8 Mattins was then at 6, Litany at 10, followed by Voluntary, Communion, and Sermon. *Clergyman's Vade-Mecum*, i. 12.

9 *Antidotum*, iii. 59.

10 Therefore there is in many places a practical convenience in having the three services close together, with no more pause than is necessary for the congregation to get into their places. For the important thing is that the congregation shall not be boxed up for the whole series, but shall be free to come and go for any of the services. This opportunity for the assembling of the congregation was assumed in the old rubric of the Commination Service,—'After mattins ended, the people being called together by the ringing of a bell and assembled in the church, the English Litany shall be said.'

11 Especially during the last half of the eighteenth century. See the list of instances in the appendix to the *Lincoln Judgement*. In 1710, however, Nicholls, in his preface to Bishop Cosin's Prayer Book, mentions the 'two wax candles' as if they were as necessary to the celebration of 'this holy rite' as the chalice and paten itself.

12 *Altar Lights and the Classification of Feasts* (S.S.O.).

13 A visit to the Flemish and Dutch rooms at the National Gallery, and to the Arundel copies of Italian pictures in the basement of the Gallery, will give the reader a good idea of the altar in the fifteenth, sixteenth, and seventeenth centuries.

14 The neglect of this duty only became universal in the worst age of sloth and pluralism. In 1688, Sancroft, in a letter to the bishops of his province, urged the public performance of the daily offices 'in all market and other great towns,' and as far as possible in less populous places. In 1714, a large proportion of the London churches had daily mattins and evensong, and week-day mattins (at 6 A.M.) was a fashionable service. (Paterson, *Pietas Londiniensis*, 305; Steele in the *Guardian* for 1713, No. 65.)

15 Blunt, 65.

16 Our rubrics allow of this substitution at any time. The Prayer Book of 1549 expressly orders the *Benedicite* to be sung in Lent instead of the *Te Deum*. The old books forbid the use of the *Te Deum* in Advent, and from *Septuagesima* till Easter.

17 It is only after the Creed that the Lord's Prayer is directed to be said 'with a loud voice.'

18 It is a good plan to vary the sentences with the season. Thus '*I acknowledge*' may be used on ordinary week-days, '*Hide thy face*' for Lent week-days, '*The sacrifices*' and '*If we say*' during Passiontide, '*Rend your heart*' on Sundays in Lent, '*To the Lord*' on Festivals, '*Repent ye*' on the Sundays in Advent, '*I will arise*' on ordinary Sundays, '*Enter not*' on Advent week-days. These occasions might be noted in the margin of the Book.

19 It is equally correct for the priest not to put on his cope till towards the end of the psalms, and for the little procession to enter just before *Magnificat*; but this is more fussy, and it seems better for the priest not to vest and unvest more than necessary.

20 There seems to be no reason why the candles should be put out till the conclusion of the service.

21 There is absolutely no authority for blessing the coins.

22 If there is another priest, it is more convenient for him to present the alms.

23 There is absolutely no authority for singing '*Let us go forth in peace.*'

24 It will be found, I think, that people keep up their attention better, because they become less weary, if it be sung in this manner. My own opinion, if I may put it forward, is that in most small churches it

is best to *say* the Litany before the principal Eucharist; and only to sing it at Rogation-tide, and then in procession.

25 On Rogation and other penitential days the procession will go by the reverse way.

CHAPTER VI
THE HOLY COMMUNION

The Lord's Supper should be celebrated at least on every Sunday and holy day, whenever there is a special collect, epistle, and gospel provided in the Prayer Book. But few devout parsons will be content with this, even in small country parishes; and the Prayer Book provides for frequent celebrations by the rubric, 'Note also that the Collect, Epistle, and Gospel, appointed for the Sunday, shall serve all the week after, where it is not in this book otherwise ordered.' For the Black-Letter days, however, it is very convenient that special collects, epistles, and gospels should be used; and most bishops would no doubt follow the present Primate's example in allowing the little book drawn up by Canon T. T. Carter and published by Masters and Co., 78 New Bond Street. For Rogation and Embertide special collects have been drawn up by authority, and they are published by the S.P.C.K. These can be bound up with the Prayer Book. For requiems the last collect but one in the burial service, containing as it does a prayer for the departed, should be used. It is a most serious breach of Catholic order to use unauthorised missals. Every effort must be made, both at sung and plain Celebrations, to obey the rubric which orders that there should be three communicants at least; and in most parishes it will be best to arrange with members of the congregation, so that there shall be some at every Mass.[1] At the same time, to omit the service because the required number do not happen to be present, would have a disastrous effect upon the faithful.[2] If the parson has done his best to comply with the rubric, and there are some present, it seems most in accord with his duty, and the rubric 'according to his discretion,' to go on with the service; but solitary Masses have always been strictly forbidden.[3] The Prayer Book rubrics as to communicants attacked the very grave evil by which, before the Reformation, attendance at the Lord's Supper had taken the place of reception, and communion only once a year had become the rule. This evil was reprobated also by the Council of Trent, which expresses a hope that some of the faithful will communicate at every Mass.

In country parishes the difficulty of getting a congregation, as well as the desire,of the priest to avoid anything like a mechanical and unprepared spirit, will often prevent the week-day celebrations being more than once or twice a week.[4] Thursday is sometimes chosen for a week-day Mass; but Thursday is the last day that should be chosen. In primitive times it was actually forbidden to celebrate on that day; it was *dies aliturgicus*. The proper days, when there are only two Celebrations, are the old station days, Wednesday and Friday; and this is, no doubt, why the Litany is ordered to be said on these two week-days.[5] If there is only one Celebration it should be on the Wednesday. The parson in a small parish, who is training his people to provide a congregation, may conveniently increase the Celebrations in something like the following order:—First, Red-Letter days, then adding Wednesday, then adding Friday, then starting the daily Celebration, which is most desirable wherever it is possible.

At the Council of London (1200) it was decreed that the priest should not celebrate twice in the day, except in case of necessity. This was explained later by Langton as including Christmas and Easter days, funerals, weddings, and the sickness or necessary absence of another priest.

It seems safer never to omit the Creed and *Gloria in Excelsis*. Yet there is a distinct case for the omission of the former on ordinary week-days, and of the latter in Advent and from Septuagesima to Easter. For it may be doubted whether the rubrics, 'shall be sung or said the Creed' and 'There shall be said or sung, *Glory*, etc.,' intended them to be sung on uncustomary occasions, when the clergy would naturally omit them. If they were to be sung on a new principle, i.e. at every Mass, one would expect some statement in the rubrics. On the contrary, however, there is a rubric at the end of the First English Prayer Book,[6] which allows of their omission, 'If there be a sermon, or for other great cause, the Curate by his discretion may leave out the Litany, *Gloria in Excelsis*, the Creed, the Homily, and the Exhortation to the Communion.' This throws a significant light on the meaning of the other rubrics; for those before the Creed and Gloria in the First Book are neither more nor less peremptory than our own. Still, in days when disobedience in many dangerous directions is so rife as at present, it seems safer, as I have said, to stick rigidly to the letter of our rubrics, if only to avoid giving a false impression of disobedience to those who are ignorant of liturgical science.

The Ten Commandments are in a different position. There is no reason for their omission without proper authority. The only excuse that I know of is the analogy of the Scotch and American Prayer Books, which allow the substitution of the Summary of the Law when the Commandments have already been said at another service, and this is a very doubtful line of defence. Moreover there is no precedent for the omission of the *Kyries*, which are an ancient feature of the beginning of the Eucharist, and farced *Kyries*,[7] such as we have in the responses to the Commandments, are also an ancient feature.

I am, of course, concerned here merely with the interpretation of existing rubrics, and not with the question whether the substitution of the ninefold *Kyrie* for the Commandments would be a useful alteration in the Prayer Book.

It is a help, when there is a special subject of intercession at the Holy Communion, to say an appropriate post-communion collect 'immediately before the Benediction.' Such collects are given in the three Ordination offices, and thus our Embertide Celebrations are provided for, and this feature sanctioned. Collects used in this way must, of course, be taken from authorised sources. It may be suggested that such collects as the following are not inappropriate, — Nineteenth Sunday after Trinity (for the Holy Spirit), Twenty-fourth Sunday (for the departed), Sixteenth or Twenty-second Sunday (for the Church), Twenty-third Sunday (for any necessity), Fifth Sunday (for peace), Good Friday (for the conversion of unbelievers and heathen), First after Epiphany (for guidance), Trinity Sunday (for special occasions of thanksgiving).

The eucharistic species are bread and wine. Wafer-bread is lawful under the present rubric, which declares only that common bread (if it be the best and purest) 'shall suffice.' It was substituted for the rubric of 1549 which enforced wafer-bread, 'unleavened, and round,' 'through all this realm, after one sort and fashion'; so that it removes the former restriction to wafer-bread, and makes both kinds lawful.[8] There is a great amount of authority in antiquity for leavened bread, and the Easterns still use it. Wafer-bread, is, however, far more convenient, and involves less risks of irreverence. A large wafer is used for the priest, and small ones for the people. Several of the sisterhoods make wafer-bread, and it is best to get it from them. Where ordinary bread is used, little machines can be bought for cutting it up into squares; but it should not be pressed. A metal box should be provided for the altar-breads.

The Judgement of the Archbishop's Court in the Lincoln Case[9] decided that the ancient rule as to the mixed chalice has never been changed, and that the use of wine alone is unlawful in the Church of England. Red wine is more in accordance with ancient custom than white, though white is rather more convenient. It should be the pure fermented juice of the grape, not doctored with alcohol, or heavily sweetened, as are so many so-called eucharistic wines. The difficulty one sometimes hears of as to persons of intemperate habits is really due to the objectionable nature of some of these wines.[10]

The Lincoln Judgement is not binding on us; but the arguments and instances which it gives are so weighty and learned that they deserve our most careful consideration. It decided that the chalice should be mixed before the service, and not at the offertory. Its reasons are, That the direction of the Prayer Book of 1549, 'putting the wine into the chalice...putting thereto a little pure and clean water,' was omitted in subsequent revisions; and that this was done 'in accordance with the highest and widest liturgical precedents.'[11] At Sarum, at high Mass, the later custom obtained, and the sub-deacon mixed the chalice after the Epistle; but at Westminster the priest mixed the chalice before the service, between the taking of the stole and chasuble; and this preparation before the service was also the custom all over England at low Mass,[12] and is still practised by the conservative Dominicans. It is certainly a sound tradition to prepare the bread and the chalice at the same time; and it gives more meaning to the solemn bringing in of the vessels which is so characteristic a feature of the English rite, as it is of those Eastern rites which have preserved the ancient customs of the Church.

If the chalice is not made in the vestry, at the beginning of the Commandments the torchbearers fetch in the cruets and basin and towel, and during the gradual the clerk makes the chalice at the credence, holding the water cruet for the priest to bless before adding water to the wine.

SUNG EUCHARIST.

It is against all ancient tradition and all old English custom, for sung Mass to be celebrated by the priest alone without the assistance of any other minister, and with only a couple of serving boys. This is a modern Roman practice, as is also the disuse of incense at what is called abroad a *Missa Cantata*.

If there are two other ministers in the church, the celebrant should be assisted by deacon and sub-deacon, and also by the clerk. If there is only one other minister in priest's or deacon's orders he should assist as deacon, and the clerk should take the duties of the sub-deacon as well as his own. If the priest is single-handed he should be assisted by the clerk, unless this is absolutely impossible.

The ancient custom was that of reverence and common sense; if there was more than one priest or deacon to show respect to the Sacrament, so much the better; but if not, then at least the clerk. Where there is no clerk and one assistant clergyman, he may do the work of the clerk as well as taking the chalice and reading the gospel and epistle. But there should always be a clerk (if possible, but not necessarily, in reader's orders); and then the assistant clergyman will take the office of deacon and the clerk add to his own duties those of sub-deacon. Even at low Mass a boy only serves in the absence of the deacon (or clerk), as is admitted by Roman authorities.

As the majority of English churches have only one priest, and as unfortunately little attempt has been made to restore his functions to the clerk, I shall give suggestions here for a Sung Eucharist at which only the priest and clerk officiate, assisted by the servers.

It need hardly be said that the man chosen for the clerk's office should be of exemplary and devout life, as well as quiet and reverent in his demeanour. His principal duties at High Mass are to carry the cross at the head of the procession, and to bear the sacred vessels to and from the sanctuary. When there is no gospeller or epistler he may also read the epistle. He should in either case wear a tunicle if possible. In those parishes where there is a reader (i.e. a person ordained by the bishop for what is curiously miscalled lay-readership), the office of clerk gives him his proper share in the service of the Church. But minor orders are not necessary for the epistler; custom long assigned to the clerk the reading of the first lesson and the epistle,[13] and a trace of this was preserved in the Prayer Book of 1549—'the priest *or he that is appointed* shall read the epistle...the minister shall read the epistle';[14] while for the gospel the deacon is specially mentioned—'the priest or one appointed to read the gospel...the priest or deacon shall then read the gospel.' Our present rubric directs the Priest to read both Epistle and Gospel, but evidently on the assumption that there is neither an epistler nor gospeller present: it was certainly so interpreted in Elizabeth's time when the rubric was new; and gospellers and epistlers are ordered for the Consecration of Bishops, the Ordering of Priests, and by Canon 24.

The persons needed for sung Mass, where there is only one priest, are these—the Priest, the Clerk, the Thurifer, and Boat-bearer, two Torchbearers; in a small place the torchbearers (or one of the torch-bearers) and thurifer might be dispensed with, but not, if possible, the clerk. It is far better for the dignity of the service not to have small boys for any office except that of boat-bearer. Let the position of server on Sundays be one that is looked up to, as something to be reached only after many years of probation; and let the boy-servers be trained and tested at the early week-day services.

In the vestry the servers will all vest in cassock, apparelled amice, and apparelled albe with girdle (or they may wear the rochet, or the surplice, but not red cassocks with semi-transparent albes).[15] Albes should be girded rather high,[16] and amices always worn with them.

To put on an apparelled amice it should be laid on a table, and given two double folds under the apparel and of the same breadth; it is then laid on the top of the head with the apparel outside, the unfolded part of the amice falling over the back of the head; the tapes, which have been hanging by either cheek, are then crossed, taken round the neck rather tightly (completely hiding the collar), and brought round to the front, when they are crossed again and brought round the back and tied round the waist. (Thus the tape which hangs down the right side is drawn to the left side of the neck and round the back till it hangs again on the right side; it then passes under the left arm, round the back of the waist to the front, where it is tied to the other. The operation is really quite as easy as putting on a collar and tie in the morning.) The amice will be kept on the head till the other vestments are on, when the apparelled edge is pulled back, so that it forms a collar standing up well outside the albe and other vestments.[17] No loops are needed on the amice, but the tapes must be about 78 in. long.

A word of general advice to the servers may be useful. The torchbearers should move together with something like a military precision; they should avoid all fuss and running about and all ostentatious reverence, still more all carelessness or irreverence; they should carry their torches in the outside hand, upright, and at an equal height. They stand throughout the service, except on the few occasions when they are directed to kneel, or when they are doing the work appointed for them. Their proper place is by and just below their torches, which are set down in their bases on the bottom step of the foot-pace (if there is room there) rather beyond the ends of the altar; except when they go into the midst of the choir for the Consecration. They must stand *still*, with their hands together, but there is no direction for them to stick their fingers out. Whenever they leave their torches they go first to the midst and bow together.

All should bow on passing the altar, except in procession. They should bow sensibly, and neither ostentatiously nor familiarly.

The thurifer, when he has put the censer away after the Offertory, will stand with his boat-bearer in some convenient place near the end of the choir stalls, till the end of the service. He should never swing the censer with its lid at all open.

The clerk, when not otherwise engaged, will stand facing north in his place, which is near the credence. He will look after the priest, giving him any music, etc., that he may want; and if anything goes wrong, as he is responsible, he will go very quietly and naturally to put it right. No one should ever whisper during service; but if anything has to be said it should be spoken quietly in the natural voice, which is much less likely to attract attention. A mistake matters little, if no one makes a fuss about it. If there is no room for another seat near the sedilia, the clerk may sit during the sermon in any convenient place.

As for the priest, he, in particular, should be quiet and dignified, as well as reverent, in his movements. He must never let his arms hang down at his sides, or his eyes wander over the congregation. He must avoid at once a jaunty and a mincing gait. He must never sidle along the altar nor stand at an undecided angle; but when he moves he must turn and walk straight, and when he stands he must face squarely in the required direction. If anything goes wrong in the singing, or among the congregation, he must not look round unless it is absolutely necessary. If he is likely to want a handkerchief, let him put a clean one in his sleeve, or tuck it in his girdle, so that he will not have to pull his albe up and search for his pocket.

If he inclines in the older fashion by bowing, he should take a step back from the altar, lay his hands on it, and bow reverently but not in an exaggerated fashion, inclining from the hips. If he genuflects, he should bring the right knee down to the ground near the left heel. The action should be without any pause, but not hurried. The hands should rest on the altar, and the head and body be kept quite erect.

If he is reverent and his thoughts intent on worship, if at the same time he is naturally graceful, and has been drilled, or taught deportment, as a boy, he will do all these things instinctively. But, as many parsons have not these qualifications, some directions are needed; for the priest occupies a prominent position in church, and faults which may be tolerable in a roomful of persons are seriously distracting and sometimes painful to the worshippers in a church. In preaching, a man with a marked individuality will do most good; but in conducting service the priest's individuality should be as unnoticeable and his actions as normal as possible. For he does not stand at the altar as Mr. A. or Mr. B., but as the minister of the people and the representative of the Church, conducting in the name of the congregation the 'Common Prayer' of them all, and administering the 'Sacraments and other Rites and Ceremonies of the Church.' The Church is sacerdotal in the true sense of that good word; but she is essentially not clericalist, and therefore she does not unduly exalt the minister by putting the people at the mercy of his own ideas of prayer, or by enthroning him at the east end of the church to overshadow the congregation. The eastward position, the sacred vestments, the chanted service, the appointed gestures, are all to hide the man and to exalt the common priesthood of the Christian congregation.

The torchbearers will light the two candles on the altar, and the two standards; they will then light their torches, and see that the socket-bases are in the right place in the sanctuary. They will also place on the credence the bason, vessel of water, and towel, if the chalice is made before the service. The thurifer will put into the censer sufficient—not too much—charcoal. The boat-bearer will see that there is incense in his boat. The clerk in his albe, but before he puts on the tunicle, will place the gospel and epistle books on the north and south ends of the altar, so that they rest against the reredos. (But if there are a deacon and sub-deacon they will carry the books themselves in procession, and carry them back at the end of the service.) Having done this, the clerk will take the processional cross from its locker, and put on his tunicle, which may be of the colour of the day, or of any colour if there are not sufficient vestments. The verger will be in readiness in his gown, his verge in his hand.

The most exact punctuality must be observed at this and at all services.

The priest will prepare the chalice, putting therein sufficient wine, to which he adds a very little water. On the chalice he will lay the folded purificator; and on the purificator the paten, containing a large wafer for himself and a sufficient number of breads for the people. On the paten he places the pall, and over all the burse containing the corporal. [At low Mass the vessels may perhaps be covered with a small veil, called a chalice-veil, before the burse is laid on the top. At low Mass also the priest carries the vessels in when he goes in to begin the service. If the chalice is already made, he must put the vessels on the credence; as by our Offertory rubric the bread and wine are not set on the table till the Offertory.] Near the table in the vestry where the vessels stand will be laid the humeral veil for the clerk.

The priest will vest in cassock, apparelled amice and albe, girdle (which is most easily tied double in a running noose), stole (crossed at the breast, and held in position by tucking the ends of the girdle round it), maniple (on left arm), and chasuble.[18] But if there is a procession (as there may be every Sunday) he wears a cope and does not put on the chasuble till after the procession. During the vesting he may say, in accordance with the ancient custom, the *Veni Creator*, and Ps. 43, *Judica me*.

The Commencement of the Service. — If there is to be a procession the priest and servers enter the chancel the short way, the choir (if there be a surpliced choir) being already in their places; arrived in the midst of the chancel, the priest blesses the incense in the usual way, and the procession starts in this order: — Verger, churchwardens, clerk in tunicle with cross, torchbearers with lighted torches, thurifer with boat-bearer at his side, celebrant in cope, choirboys, choir-men, other clergy in surplice, hood, and tippet.[19] When it has returned, the priest goes off with the torchbearers, thurifer, and clerk by the short way to the vestry, where he changes his cope for a chasuble. Where there is no vestry near enough, the chasuble may be put on at the altar. The choir sing the Introit. The priest, having put on the chasuble, goes with the servers into the choir as when there is no procession.

If there be no procession, the priest and servers start at the commencement of the introit (which may consist of the old verses appointed from holy Scripture, or of the psalms set down in the Prayer Book of 1549),[20]going to the altar the long way,[21] in the following order: — Verger, clerk with cross, torch-bearers, thurifer and boat-bearer, priest (saying to himself as he goes Psalm 43).

When the priest has arrived at the foot of the altar steps, all bow; the torchbearers then set down their torches in the usual place,[22] the clerk puts the cross down in a convenient place (against the north wall of the sanctuary is best), and stands near the credence. The thurifer remains still for a while, the verger goes to the sacristy by the short way and waits there. The priest then goes up to the altar, and, bending forward with hands joined, prays silently, kisses the altar in the midst.[23] The thurifer has followed him and remains standing behind him: the priest turns to the right, the clerk comes up to the thurifer, and taking the spoon, puts incense into the censer; the priest then blesses the incense, and, receiving the censer from the thurifer, censes the altar[24] in the midst and at the south and north sides, taking the ring in his left hand, and grasping the chains near the cover with his right. Going back to the south of the altar, he then gives the censer to the clerk, and remains standing in the same place while the clerk censes him. The clerk then gives the censer to the thurifer, who takes it to the vestry and hangs it on a peg. Turning to the altar[25] the priest alone says the Lord's Prayer, with its *Amen*, without note but quite audibly; he says the Collect for Purity in the same way, but the people take up the *Amen*, though still without note.

He then, 'turning to the, people,' where he stands (not going to the middle), rehearses 'distinctly' on a note the Ten Commandments, the people singing the *Kyrie* after each Commandment.

At the conclusion of the last *Kyrie*, the priest turns back to the altar, and 'standing as before' says one of the Collects for the Queen. Thus the Preparation, Commandments, and Collect for the Queen are all said in the same place.

As the first *Kyrie* is being sung, the torchbearers take up their torches, and, without bowing, walk straight to the chancel steps, where they stand facing one another. The clerk, meanwhile, has placed the humeral veil on his shoulders, his left hand in the left end of the veil holds the stem of the chalice; holding the other end of the veil with his right hand over the top of the burse, he carries the sacred vessels to the altar, going the long way. He walks solemnly and slowly, holding the vessels breast high. He is thus met at the chancel gates by the torch-bearers, who precede him to the sanctuary step, where they stand, holding their candles. The clerk, after passing between them, turns to the right, walks along the pavement till he is in a line with the credence, then turns again, goes up to the credence, and sets the vessels upon it. The clerk removes his humeral veil, and he may spread it on the vessels. He then takes the burse and carries it solemnly to the altar steps, walks straight up to the midst of the altar and then sets the burse down, leaning it against the reredos with its closed edge downwards. As the clerk comes down the steps the torchbearers replace their torches in the bases.

The Collect, Epistle, and Gospel. 'Then shall be said the Collect for the Day,' the priest going for this to the south[26] side if he has said the Preparation, etc., at the north. (It is best in this case for the Book to be laid on the south cushion before the commencement of the service; and for the priest to say the Preparation, etc., from memory, or with the aid of a small book.) The Prayer Book gives no rule as to the collects being of an uneven number (which was not a universal custom); but it orders a second collect for Lent and Advent, and three for Good Friday; a memorial may no doubt be also added when there is a concurrence of festivals, or some special object of prayer, and one of the collects at the end of the Communion Service may be said 'after the collects either of Morning or Evening Prayer, Communion, or Litany, by the discretion of the Minister.'

The priest will say all the prayers facing due east, his hands slightly extended, so that the elbows touch the sides, and the palms face each other with fingers united, but not exceeding the height or limit of the shoulders: at the concluding sentence of the prayers he joins his hands.

If the priest is to read the Epistle, there is no good reason why he should not turn to the people. Such is undoubtedly the spirit of the Prayer Book, such has always been the custom since the Mass has been said in English. At low Mass, when it was in Latin, it was the custom to say it facing east, which was reasonable enough, as the people could not understand it; but now that they can, they resent its being said away from them, and thus unnecessary difficulties are put in the Church's way. In the Sarum Missal there is no direction. And 'in the early *Ordines* and liturgical writers we find no trace of reading the Gospel or Epistle with back to the people' (Dr. W. Legg, *S.P.E.S. Trans.* ii. 125). Le Brun himself in the *Explication de la Messe* praises the Armenians for preserving the ancient custom of singing the Epistle towards the people, and says in another place, 'L'usage ancien et le plus naturel est que tout le monde écoute le soudiacre' (cf. *Notes on Ceremonial*, p. 183).

If the clerk is to read the Epistle, the priest goes by the short way to the sedilia immediately after the collect, and sits down; the torchbearers leave their torches and sit by him. The clerk then takes the book of the epistles from the altar, and goes to the choir, when he stands near the entrance on the south side, facing the people.

Both the Gospel and Epistle should be sung to the old tones, with due regard to their rhythm and meaning, or else recited on a note.

The Epistle is begun with the words, '*The Epistle (or the portion of Scripture appointed for the Epistle) is written in the — Chapter of — beginning at the — verse.*' 'And the Epistle ended, he shall say, *Here endeth the Epistle.*' Then the gradual (and tract or sequence),[27] or a suitable hymn, may be sung.

During the gradual the clerk goes to the altar, takes the corporal from the burse, and spreads it on the altar. Towards the end of the gradual the priest rises, and, preceded by the clerk, goes the short way to the midst of the altar. The thurifer approaches, the clerk puts incense into the censer, the priest blesses the incense, takes the censer and censes the midst of the altar. Meanwhile the clerk preceded by the torchbearers (who carry their torches) walks round to the north end of the altar and there stands facing south, the torchbearers on either side of him facing each other: the thurifer having received the censer back from the priest, follows them, and stands behind the clerk (or, if the chancel be small, in some convenient place), gently swinging the censer. On festivals the clerk holds the cross during the gospel; on other occasions he may stand with his hands together. As he announces the gospel, the priest signs the book and then himself on the forehead and breast, but not on the mouth. The choir turn east and sing '*Glory be to Thee, O Lord,*' but the priest *remains facing north.* The servers should not sign themselves or bow when they are holding torch, thurible, or cross.

'Then shall he read the Gospel (the people all standing up) saying, *The holy Gospel is written in the — Chapter of — beginning at the — verse.*' The Gospel will be read by the priest himself [unless there is a deacon assisting, when the priest stands at the south side of the altar] at the north part of the altar facing north, the book resting on the altar.

At the conclusion of the Gospel the choir, still facing east, sing '*Praise be to Thee, O Christ,*' or '*O Lord.*' This usage, though in no English missal, can be traced in England to the seventeenth century, and probably had come down to us by tradition. It is ordered in the Scotch liturgy and sanctioned by the 29th of the present Scotch Canons. The priest kisses the book at the conclusion of the Gospel.

Himself moving the cushion and missal from the north to near the centre, so that it lies just to the north of the corporal, the priest begins the Creed. If he is strong enough, it is more in accordance with the spirit of English worship that he should stand while the Creed is being sung. If not, he may go with the torchbearers (whose torches of course remain in their bases) to the sedilia, after privately reciting the Creed. All bow at the Holy Name; at the *Incarnatus* the choir bow, the priest, servers, and people may either bow or kneel.[28]

'Then shall the Curate declare unto the people what Holy-days, or Fasting-days, are in the week following to be observed,' etc. 'Then shall follow the Sermon' (cap. vii.). If the celebrant is to give out the notices, he will do so, in his chasuble, from the altar step; but if he is also to preach, he takes off his chasuble and maniple, spreading them on the south side of the altar, and then enters the pulpit. If he preaches in his chasuble from the altar step, he will probably offend the congregation and preach badly. If the sermon is to be preached by another priest, it is generally more convenient that he too should give out the notices. He remains in his stall till the verger comes to fetch him, which the latter will do towards the end of the Creed.

The Banns of Marriage should be published with the notices; 'immediately before the sentences for the Offertory,' are the words of the Prayer Book, inserted in 1662, when often there was no sermon. The rubric now generally printed at the beginning of the Marriage Service, ordering the banns to be published during morning service, or at evening service, if there be no morning service, has been inserted without authority, and one of the testimonies of the Prayer Book to the need of a weekly Eucharist thereby removed. It is simply a statement from an ambiguous Act of Parliament, of 26 Geo. II., about which lawyers have not agreed.

There is some difficulty as to the notice of the Communion. The rubric after the Creed orders it to be given with the other notices, but only 'if occasion be'; so that it need not be given unless the curate feels it to be necessary.[29] But the 'Warning for the celebration of the holy Communion,' which is printed after the Church Militant Prayer, is to be given 'after the Sermon or Homily ended,' and not where it is printed. It is generally taken as included under the phrase 'if occasion be'; so, of course, is the Exhortation to the Negligent. The Third Exhortation might be only read occasionally, following its use under the First Book.[30] They are all too long for ordinary use; and custom, and the Ordinary, allow their omission. Nevertheless their teaching is often needed; and the Warning, especially, with its call to Confession, may well be read on the Sunday before the great Festivals, at least before Easter, when all communicate, and perhaps also before Christmas and Whitsunday, which are practically the other days of general communion.

The Offertory. The Sermon over, the priest goes to the midst of the altar, and, facing east, says on a note 'one or more' of the Sentences, to 'begin the Offertory.' Meanwhile the torchbearers go to the credence and stand facing north. Usually one sentence only is said, and is immediately followed by a hymn or anthem, which should be fairly long if there is to be the censing of persons and things. This is a very suitable place for an anthem. It is well to make the Sentences speak as much as possible of the season, and but little of money; therefore a selection may be made. *'Let your light'* is suitable for Saints' Days; *'Whatsoever ye would,'* by its comprehensiveness, for ordinary occasions; *'Not every one'* for the great feasts; *'While we have time,'* on occasions of special intercession for the living or departed. If a rule like this is kept to, the people soon learn to appreciate its significance, and the Offertory Sentence is used in the ancient spirit.

'While these sentences are in reading, the Deacons, Churchwardens, or other fit persons...shall receive the alms...in a decent bason.' The best way to carry out the rubric in most churches is for the wardens and sidesmen to collect the alms (which no one must be suffered to call the 'offertory') in wooden plates[31] (or bags, so that they be not of the colour of the season); the collection finished, they put their plates on the large bason which is held by the clerk [in the absence of a deacon] at the chancel-gates. The clerk carries the bason up to the altar (not hanging behind out of the priest's sight), and shall 'reverently bring it to the priest, who shall humbly present and place it upon the holy Table.' The priest 'presents' the alms by slightly raising the bason (without any signing) and then placing it upon the holy Table on the right of the corporal, whence it will be removed by the clerk.

Then, after the alms have been presented, the real Offertory should now begin. The clerk, putting on the humeral veil with the assistance of the torch-bearers, takes the chalice and the paten, covered with a pall, and gives them to the priest, who 'shall then place upon the Table,' and then raise them slightly together (the paten lying on the chalice) as an offering to God. Then he places the paten on the corporal immediately in front of the chalice,[32] and he covers the chalice with the pall. (If a ciborium is necessary it will be placed on the altar by the clerk immediately after the chalice and paten.)

The priest then takes the censer, and censes the oblations, first making three signs of the cross with the censer over them, then swinging the censer thrice round them, and then giving one swing on each side of them. He does not cense the altar. The clerk takes the censer from him, and goes to the pavement on the south side, and, turning to the priest, censes him. They bow to each other slightly, both before and after the censing, as is customary. The thurifer then takes the censer from the clerk and 'censes the choir,' in grades, first on the Decani then on the Cantoris side, —which is all the direction the Sarum Missal gives.[33] Perhaps this is best done in the most simple way, by the thurifer turning west where he stands, and swinging the censer towards the south-west and north-west. He then takes the censer out, accompanied always by the boat-bearer, and puts it away; they return to the choir and remain in their place for the rest of the service.

Meanwhile the torchbearers, who have been standing near the credence since the offertory sentence, come to the priest at the north end of the altar; one, holding the basin, pours water over his fingers, the other presents to him the towel. The priest according to the Sarum rite would here say to himself, 'Cleanse me, O God, from every stain of mind and body, that I may in purity fulfil the holy work of the Lord,' but no psalm. The torchbearer at once pours the water down the piscina.

The priest goes to the midst of the altar; and, after turning to the people[34] to say, *'Let us pray for the whole state,…'* he says the Church Militant Prayer facing east and with extended hands as usual.

In the Church Militant Prayer is part of the old Canon. The first clause, down to *'truth, unity, and concord,'* is a paraphrase of the *Te igitur*; therefore, following the ancient ritual, the oblations may be signed[35] when they are mentioned (but not the alms). The long clause from *'And grant'* to *'any other adversity'* is a paraphrase of the *Memento Domine*; therefore slight, but very slight, pauses may be made during which the priest remembers any for whom he wishes specially to pray. The next clause *'And we also bless'* is a paraphrase of *Communicantes*, a commemoration of the Saints; and *'beseeching thee to give'* contains the prayer of *Hanc igitur*.[36]

'Then shall the Priest say to them that come to receive the holy Communion, *Ye that do truly.*' At a sung Celebration the Invitation is said in a quiet but audible voice and without a note. It is addressed only to those who intend to communicate; and it will be much more seemly and convenient if they are placed together somewhere near the chancel gates,[37] 'the Communicants being conveniently placed for the receiving of the holy Sacrament.'

'Then shall this general Confession be made, in the name of all those that are minded to receive the holy Communion, by one of the Ministers; both he and all the people kneeling humbly upon their knees, and saying...' The meaning of this rubric seems to be clear that—(1) The Confession is to be said by the deacon or sub-deacon, or in the service which we are describing by the clerk their substitute. (2) He who leads the Confession need not be an intending communicant, for his office is clearly only to say it 'in the name' of the communicants. (3) Not the clerk only and the communicants, but 'all the people,' are to join in the Confession. As they are to kneel 'humbly,' they are also presumably to speak humbly; and the unseemliness of saying the Confession on a note is to be avoided. It is far the most impressive way for the clerk to say the words quietly but clearly, so that he can keep the congregation together, while they follow him in a low murmur; as choir-boys are often not confirmed, and as they have an incurable tendency to get on to a note, it is better (both here and at the Confession at Mattins and Evensong) for them to be silent.[38]

As the next rubric, 'Then shall the Priest stand up,' was carried bodily from the Book of 1549, it is perhaps open to doubt whether he is meant to kneel unless he leads the Confession himself. It seems safer, however, for him to kneel.

'Then shall the Priest (or the Bishop, being present) stand up, and turning himself to the people, pronounce this Absolution,' still in a natural voice. He should raise his right hand at '*Have mercy upon you*,' but he must not make the sign of the Cross. The Lincoln Judgement points, out that neither in the uses of Sarum, York, nor Hereford is there any direction for making the sign of the Cross at absolutions. It is 'borrowed and introduced from foreign usages' (though even in the Roman missal the priest signs himself only), and is in no 'sense a continuance of old prescription in the Church of England.'[39]

'Then shall the Priest,' still turned towards the people, and with hands joined, 'say, *Hear what comfortable words*...' The Comfortable Words may be said with or without a note, or sung.

The Preface. As he sings '*Lift up your hearts*,' the priest extends and slightly raises his hands; he joins them again at '*Let us give thanks*.' When the choir (standing eastward) has finished the response, 'Then shall the Priest turn to the Lord's Table, and say' the Preface (with a Proper Preface, if one be appointed in the Prayer Book) with extended hands. The choir sing the *Sanctus*, during which the priest, according to the Sarum Missal, should 'raise his arms a little and join his hands,' which seems to mean that his joined fingers are just beneath his chin. When the choir sing the *Benedictus*[40] he signs himself at the words '*in the name of the Lord.*'

The short pause for private prayer should not be made here, but after the Prayer of Humble Access. But at a sung service such prayer may be said during the *Sanctus* and *Benedictus*, which should be sung together, and not separated by the Prayer of Access. There is absolutely no authority for the quite modern Continental custom of separating the *Benedictus* from the *Sanctus*.

At the *Sanctus* the torchbearers leave their torches and go out of the sanctuary to the midst of the choir, where they stand side by side, facing east. They kneel during the Prayer of Access, and bow reverently (not kneel) during the Consecration, bowing also whenever the priest bows or kneels. When the Priest turns to communicate the people, they genuflect where they stand, and go off to the right and left, when they stand in a convenient place near the altar rails. When the communion of the people is finished, they return to the sanctuary, and, after genuflecting together, go off right and left to their torches.

There is no direction in the Sarum books for any use of incense, or entry or lifting of torches, at the Consecration. Incense and torches were, however, used in some other places.[41] The old spirit of keeping a solemn silence, with nothing to distract either priest, servers, or congregation, at this supreme moment, is surely the most fitting as it is the most impressive. The priest and ministers stand alone in the sanctuary, from which the servers have reverently withdrawn; all stand like watchers round the sacred presence, with bodies inclined, having no distracting thoughts as to what they are to do next to keep them from prayer and worship. Fuss is nothing less than irreverence. Perhaps the bell in the tower will toll three times at each consecration, and a small bell may also be used if it is felt to be desirable.[42]

At the Prayer of Humble Access, 'the Priest, kneeling down at the Lord's Table,' says the words in his natural voice. The people reply *Amen* quietly and without a note. The priest at once stands.

The Consecration. If there is a standing pyx containing extra breads, or a second chalice, the priest will, before commencing the

Consecration Prayer, so order them 'that he may with the more readiness and decency' consecrate them 'before the people.' This phrase 'before the people' was inserted by the Revisers of 1662, and that demanded by the Puritan Divines, 'in the sight of the people,' deliberately rejected.

After a pause for private prayer, he says the Consecration Prayer clearly and quite audibly, but humbly, solemnly, and in his natural voice. The clause *'Grant that we receiving'* being a rendering of *Quam Oblationem*, he may make the old signs over the elements, once at *'creatures'* once at *'bread'* and at *'wine'* and at *'body'* and *'blood'* reverently regarding the oblations the while. At the words *'took bread,'* 'here the Priest is to take the Paten into his hands,' he slightly raises the paten with both hands and looks upwards. Then he takes the large bread, that he may at the words *'he brake it'* 'break the bread.' After the next sentence he lays his right 'hand upon all the bread' and says clearly and distinctly, *'this is my Body which is given for you.'* He then inclines.[43] He then elevates the Sacrament with both hands, saying as he does so,[44] *'Do this in remembrance of me.'* After this he inclines again. According to very ancient custom he will not now disjoin the finger and thumb of either hand till the ablutions, except to touch the Bread.

At the words *'took the Cup,'* 'here he is to take the Cup into his hand,'[45] — first removing the pall — holding it with both hands, and slightly raising it. At the words *'for this is my Blood,'* he is 'to lay his hand upon every vessel,' finishing the words without break down to *'sins.'* He then inclines as before, and slightly elevates[46] the Chalice as he says, *'Do this as oft as ye shall drink it in remembrance of me.'* He then inclines as before.[47]

The choir sing the Amen, which has here a special significance. They then sing the *Agnus*, after which a Communion Hymn may be sung.

The priest occupies the interval with his own private prayers, preparation, and communion. This interval, both at high and low Mass, is necessary, and is by no means an innovation: if it be not too long, it is also very helpful to the people. Many clergy will naturally prefer to form their own private prayers on the old lines; but even in their private devotions it is well to remember how much of the old prayers are still in our Book, and to avoid repetitions. *Supra quae* and *Supplices*, for instance, have been rendered at the commencement of the Consecration Prayer and in the Prayer of Access; and their inappropriateness *after* the Consecration has been admitted by many liturgical writers of authority.[48] The *Paternoster*, again, is to be said after the Communion; and even the prayer for the departed finds a public place in our liturgy, for the words *'and all thy whole Church,'* in the Prayer of Oblation, can only be logically interpreted as including the faithful departed, for which reason a short pause may well be made at the conclusion of the phrase.

It is essential that the celebrant communicate. After he has communicated, he places the pall on 'the chalice, having first passed his thumb along the edge to dry it. He then inclines, takes the paten (or pyx, if there be many communicants), goes to the south side of the altar rails, and proceeds to communicate 'the people also in order, into their hands,' not into their fingers; they should hold up the palm of their right hand, putting the palm of the left under it, — which is the godly and decent order of the ancient Fathers.[49] Returning to the altar he puts the paten on the corporal, inclines, removes the pall, and, taking up the chalice, goes to the altar rails. [If there is a deacon the priest gives him the chalice before he takes the paten himself.] The traditional method with us of 'delivering' the Cup into the hands of the people, is, in my opinion, by far the safest and most reverent way of administering it. It is very difficult to guide the chalice, unless the people take it themselves; and many resent the apparent want of trust when the minister refuses to let go of it. The communicant should grasp it firmly with *both* hands. The priest will be careful to repeat the whole formula of administration to each communicant.

Post-Communion. After the Communion, he unfolds the pall (which is really a second corporal), and spreads it over the Chalice and Paten; according to the rubric 'to return to the Lord's Table, and reverently place upon it what remaineth of the consecrated Elements, covering the same with a fair linen cloth.'

The torchbearers return to their usual place, and remain standing. The clerk still stands by the credence.

He then chants the *Paternoster*, in the midst of the altar, with hands extended, the choir joining in. In the same position he says the Prayer of Oblation. There is an alternative prayer, that of Thanksgiving, which seems to be suitable at times of general communion. He then chants *'Glory be to God on high,'* the choir joining in; he joins his hands at the next clause and keeps them joined. All bow at *'we praise Thee,'* at *'receive our prayer,'* and at the end, signing themselves.

He then inclines, steps a little to the north of the midst of the altar, and turns to the. people to say the blessing, his left hand still resting on the altar. He says the *Pax, facing the people*,[50] raising his right hand to the level of his face, —all the fingers (except the first) being straight out and joined—till '*Amen*.' He does not make the sign of the cross. The clerk and torchbearers kneel at the blessing.

Turning back to the altar, he inclines once, and then 'immediately after the Blessing' consumes what remains of the Blessed Sacrament.[51] He may, if it be necessary, call on some of those who have just communicated to assist in this, 'reverently.'[52]

The priest first consumes what remains of the Sacrament of the Body; he then carefully wipes the paten with his finger, holding it over the chalice. Without any more inclinations he drinks what remains in the chalice.

The priest then takes the Ablutions, this being the only possible way of entirely consuming what remains of the consecrated Elements.[53]

The method is as follows[54]: —

1. The priest goes to the south side, carrying the chalice and paten, his fingers still joined; he holds out the chalice for the wine, which the clerk [or sub-deacon] pours in, and drinks it from the same part of the chalice that has been previously used.[55]

2. He then holds the bowl of the chalice with the three last fingers of both hands, laying the thumb and forefinger of each hand over the bowl, so that the minister can pour water over them into the chalice: he then holds the paten (and ciborium) for water to be poured into it, and empties it into the chalice; after which he drinks this ablution of water.

The priest will be careful, of course, to see that all that part of the chalice which has been used is rinsed. He should drink the ablutions facing east, carefully, but without lifting the chalice higher than necessary.

He then takes the vessels to the midst of the Holy Table, wipes the chalice and paten with the purificator; lays the purificator on the chalice, and places the paten on the top. He then folds the pair of corporals, puts them into the burse, and lays the burse on the top of the paten.

The clerk meanwhile has put on the humeral veil and approached the altar by the midst. He stands at the right of the priest, who gives him the sacred vessels. Muffling his hands in the ends of the veil as before, the clerk takes the vessels and carries them solemnly out the long way, preceded by the torchbearers with their torches. They stand at the chancel-gates for him to pass, and then return for the priest: he comes down the steps, and bows with the torchbearers. The thurifer and boat-bearer stand behind them to bow, and then they all return to the sacristy the long way, preceded by the clerk who has returned the short way for his cross. There may be no objection to the priest saying the first fourteen verses of St. John's Gospel to himself as he goes out.[56]

After the last hymn (which is generally sung during the ablutions) is finished, the choir go out.

Arrived in the sacristy or vestry, the priest may say a prayer before unvesting (a suitable one is 'O God, who in this wonderful sacrament has left us a memorial of thy Passion; grant us, we beseech thee, so to venerate the sacred Mysteries of thy Body and Blood, that we may ever feel within ourselves the fruit of thy Redemption. Who livest,' etc.). He then unvests, first putting the amice over his head; afterwards, he goes in his cassock back to the church to say his thanksgiving. All the vestments should be carefully laid down, and not thrown in disorder. The clerk will see that everything is put away, and the torchbearers will put out the lights.

Deacon and Sub-deacon. If there is a deacon assisting, as well as the clerk, his duties will be as follows: —He walks in next before the priest; puts the incense into the censer; censes the celebrant. His usual position is on the step next below the footpace, at the right of the priest. He sits during the Epistle on the right of the priest. Towards the end of the Gradual, he goes the short way to the altar, spreads the corporal, then puts incense in the censer, and censes the Gospel-book as it lies by the corporal in the midst of the altar. He then takes the book and follows the other ministers to the gospel lectern, which stands on the north side of the choir near the gates. Having sung or said the Gospel, facing north (or west, if it be convenient), he hands the book to the clerk (who places it on the credence), and stands at his usual place.

He stands at the right-hand of the priest while the latter reads the Offertory sentence; he then takes the chalice and paten from the clerk and hands them to the priest. He puts incense into the censer; and, when the priest has censed the oblations, he censes the priest. He hands the alms-bason to the priest; and then stands at his usual post, turning, kneeling and inclining with the priest. He may lead the confession. He genuflects before taking the chalice to communicate the people, and after giving it back to the priest. When the priest is taking the ablutions, he goes up and folds the corporals. He receives the vessels from the priest, covers them with the burse, and hands them to the clerk.

For more elaborate directions, *Notes on Ceremonial* might be consulted.[57]

The principal duties of the sub-deacon are to read the Epistle (after receiving the book from the clerk) from the south side of the choir near the gates; to hold the Gospel-book for the deacon; to hand the vessels to the deacon, and to pour the water over the priest's fingers; and to give the priest the wine and water for the ablutions. He walks before the deacon. His usual position is on the step below the deacon, behind him at the first part of the service, and on the left of the priest from the offertory till the end of the service.

Notes

1 We are sometimes told that the word 'Mass' should not be used because it arouses prejudice; and the advice may often be useful. But, in a book like this which is written for reasonable people, it would not be right to respect a prejudice at once so illogical and uncharitable. 'The Lord's Supper,' 'Mass,' 'Communion,' 'Eucharist,' are different names for one and the same thing, and to talk of 'abolishing the Mass' is as stupidly blasphemous as it would be to talk of abolishing the Lord's Supper. Indeed, the Reformation was brought about in England on the distinct understanding that the Mass should not be 'abolished.' In the First Prayer Book the convenient popular title is preserved—'commonly called the Mass.' In 1549, Edward VI. solemnly assured the Devonshire rebels that 'as to the Mass, the King assures them the learned clergy have taken a great deal of pains to settle that point, to strike off innovations, and bring it back to our Saviour's institution.'—Collier, ii. 271.

2 Cosin, who approved of the rule so much that he inserted it in his Durham Prayer Book, certainly held this to be its intention. 'Better were it,' he wrote, 'to endure the absence of the people than for the minister to neglect the usual and daily sacrifice of the Church, by

which all people, whether they be there or no, reap so much benefit. And this was the opinion of my lord and master, Dr. Overall,' —who wrote the last part of the Catechism. (*Works*, v. 127.)

3 Indeed the medieval rule was that three or at least two should be present. Even in 1528 a writer says, '*Nullus presbyterorum missarum solennia celebrare presumat nisi duobus presentibus et sibi respondentibus,*' because the priest addresses the congregation in the plural '*vobiscum*' and '*fratres.*' *S.P.E.S. Trans.* ii. 124.

4 It was never considered necessary in England for priests to celebrate every day: *e.g.* St. Thomas of Canterbury, Colet, and others quoted by the Roman writer, Rev. T. E. Bridgett, in his *History of the Holy Eucharist*, ii. 132.

5 In the First Prayer Book the Litany is distinctly ordered to be said on Wednesdays and Fridays, and at its conclusion the priest to vest for Mass.

6 The rubrics in the American office are, 'Then shall be said or sung, all standing, *Gloria in Excelsis*, or some proper Hymn from the Selection,' and, 'But the Creed may be omitted, if it hath been said immediately before in Morning Prayer; provided that the Nicene Creed shall be said on Christmas-day, Easter-day, Ascension-day, Whitsun-day, and Trinity-Sunday.'

7 For ancient examples see—Maskell, *Ancient Liturgy*, 109; Blunt, 166; *Missale Sarum*, 929-933.

8 'Its wording "it shall suffice" seems to indicate non-enforcement rather than suppression of the old custom, sanctioned in the older Rubric; and this was certainly the view taken in the Injunctions of 1559 and correspondence thereon.' Bp. Barry, *Teacher's Prayer Book* (*in loc.*). Wafer-bread was frequently used in the reigns of Elizabeth and James I. Charles Leslie in the time of Queen Anne said that some clergy always used unleavened bread (*Works*, i. 511).

9 *Read* v. *Bishop of Lincoln*, p. 13.

10 Suitable wines are sold by Ford and Son, 409 Oxford Street.

11 *Ibid*. p. 11. A vast number of instances illustrating this point can be found in Dr. W. Legg's 'Comparative Study of the Time at which the Elements are prepared.' *S.P.E.S. Trans*. iii.

12 *Low Mass in England*. Rev. A. S. Barnes (S. S. Osmund).

13 Archbishop Grindal (1575) requires that persons appointed to the office of parish-clerk should be able and ready to read the first lesson and epistle as is used. Grindal, *Remains*, 142-168. Cf. Robertson *On the Liturgy* (cap. 10), also for note as to the admission of those to read who were not in minor orders, in ancient times. A few traces of this have come down to our times; *e.g.* the parish-clerk at Christ Church, Hants, 'has from time immemorial worn a surplice, and has up to quite recent times read the lessons and the epistle.' (What sacerdotalist robbed him of his duties?) This vesting of the clerk can be traced back in other places—*e.g.* in the Churchwarden's Account Book at All Saints, Hereford, occurs in 1619 the entry, 'One surplesse for the minister, and one surplesse for the clarke.' Canon 91 requires that the clerk be competent to read, write, and sing.

14 'With the first Liturgy of Edward VI. the clerk was to read the Epistle. In the companion to the first book, plainly written for the use of the clerk, and published by Grafton under the name of "Psalter" in 1549, the priest or the clerk is to read the epistle. See an article by 'J. W. L.' in the *Church Times* for December 2, 1898, which appeared since the above was written, and gives a list of authorities from 'the ninth century to the nineteenth.'

15 The servers should never wear gloves; which are an objectionable bit of fancy ritual, and are forbidden even by Baldeschi. They can easily be taught to wash their hands before the service. Red slippers are not to be commended.

16 Anciently the albe was pulled over the girdle to reduce it to the required length. But we have not yet succeeded in making this arrangement graceful.

17 The apparel is tacked on to the amice on all sides, not on the top side only; as it is not meant to fall down in the shape of an Eton collar.

18 If the proper vestments are not worn, the priest had better wear surplice and stole only, and not the hood. But an ample plain chasuble without orphreys can be used almost everywhere without rousing ignorant prejudice.

19 *i.e.*, a visitor or special preacher. Any clergy attached to the church should assist as sacred ministers, even if the church has no dalmatics; for in that case it is in accordance with ancient precedent for the deacon to wear over his albe and amice a stole crossed under the right arm and maniple, and the sub-deacon a maniple but not a

stole. When the church possesses only one dalmatic it should, according to precedent, be worn by the deacon, if there is one, the other ministers being in albes, etc.

20 The use of a whole psalm for the introit is the more ancient custom (Gasquet, 190). It is also more convenient; and, being the use of the First Prayer Book, has more authority for us.

21 The 'long way' is when the chancel is entered from the west; the 'short way' is when it is entered by a side entrance on the north or south.

22 In some churches, during the singing of the introit, the priest and torchbearers here privately confess to and absolve one another, the torchbearers kneeling close to the priest. The old prayers are correctly given in *Servers' Ceremonial* (Pickering, 9d.), which is useful for servers. It will be noticed that the English form is shorter and better than the Roman one. At low Celebrations it seems better that any preparation should be over before the bell has ceased ringing, so that the *Paternoster* may be begun at the last stroke of the bell.

23 'To kiss the Lord's table,' 'shifting of the book,' 'sacrying bells,' and altar lights, were all forbidden together by certain 'Articles' *after* the Act of Uniformity of 1549.

24 The Sarum books have only these simple directions: at Mass the direction is, '*primo in dextera, secundo in sinistra parte, et interim in medio,*' at Vespers, '*primo in medio, deinde in dextera parte, post in sinistra.*' In some copies of some parts of the Customary the directions are *ter in media, ter in sinistra,* and *ter in dextera parte.* (See Frere, 183). The arrangement of the medieval altar would also lead us to suppose that the elaborate and intricate method of censing employed by the Roman Church in modern times was unknown.

25 I leave open the vexed question as to whether the priest should stand at the north or south of the altar. The *Lincoln Judgement* in a very thorough statement of the case left this matter open, while declaring the eastward position throughout the service to be legal. It declared the words in the rubric, 'standing at the north side,' to be abrogated by the changed position of the Holy Table; and that for the priest to stand at the northern part of the front could not be regarded as a fulfilment of the rubric, but 'only as an accommodation of the rubric to the present position of the Table.' In favour, however, of the north part may be urged that this position was taken by a good many after the Savoy Conference when the north end had been

condemned by the Bishops. The north end has never been authorised since [*Lincoln Judgement*, p. 34], but the north part of the front was used at St. Paul's in 1681, and in other ways is shown to have had high sanction [*Ibid.* 116-121]. Neither is this commencing the service at the north part of the front an innovation: it was done at Westminster Abbey in the middle ages, and is still the custom of the Carthusians. On the other hand, the south part was undoubtedly the proper place in parish churches before the Reformation, and it was so ordered in the Sarum Missal ('*in dextero cornu*'); it is therefore urged that, as the altar now stands in its old position against the east wall, the priest should also resume his old position at the southern part. It has been proposed that the Preparation to the end of the Commandments should be said below the altar, the priest then going up to the altar at the south side for the Collect for the Queen. But this cannot be done; for it crosses the rubric at the beginning of this Collect, 'standing as before.'

26 Up to the last revision the Collect for the King followed the Collects for the day under one *Let us pray*: they would therefore all be said in one place. Now that there is a distinct break, and a fresh rubric which includes Collect, Epistle, and Gospel together, and directs the Epistle to be said 'immediately after the Collect,' it seems better to cross over before the Collect for the Day; and this is much more convenient when the Epistle is read at the altar.

27 A collection of sequences is published by the Plainsong Music Society, 9 Berners Street, W.

28 The Sarum rubric ordering a bow refers only to choir; the Hereford missal does not mention the choir, but has '*fiet genuflexio*' and '*tunc fiet levatio*.' But in many places the priest bowed. See *Low Mass in England* (S.S.O.), 10.

29 This agrees perfectly with the wording of the rubric, '*When* the Minister giveth warning... (which he shall always do upon the Sunday, or some Holy-day immediately preceding)'; the point of the phrase in brackets being, not that he shall always give warning, but that when he does do so it shall be done on the Sunday or Holy-day before, and not in a semi-private manner on an ordinary week-day.

30 In the First Prayer Book (pp. 70 and 172) two rubrics allow the third Exhortation to be omitted (1) on week days, (2) when there is a sermon, (3) for other great cause; so that there is very little occasion left for its reading. In cathedrals it was to be read once a month; and

the other exhortation was everywhere only for occasional use. It seems more loyal to the Prayer Book, if we use this Third Exhortation thus occasionally, as it was originally directed to be used. Indeed it is probable that they are all only meant for occasional use, like those pre-Reformation exhortations from which they are taken.

31 On special occasions the rubric may well be followed by the deacons and clerk leaving the chancel and taking the collection themselves. This generally has a good result.

32 Our rubric does not admit of the paten being slipped under the corporal.

33 There are further directions in the Consuetudinary. But the 'choir' meant only the clergy in choir, which looks as if in an ordinary parish church the thurifer would take the censer out of the chancel directly after the censing of the celebrant.

The deacon was directed at some occasions to walk right round the altar, swinging the censer, before giving it up to the thurifer. But this direction is not given at the Mass. Both Missal and Customary speak of a censing *in circuitu*, but it is the relics not the altar that are censed,—which abrogates that ceremony for us. Comp. *Missale Sarum*, 595 (and note), *Consuetudinary and Customary* (Frere), 44, 77, 114, 183.

34 The First Prayer Book has the direction here, 'turn him to the people' and then 'turning him to the altar,' which establishes the tradition. Usually the priest turns by his right to face the people, and turns back the same way, but at the *Orate fratres* he turned right round, finishing the second half-turn after he had addressed the people; and this seems to stand in its place.

35 Such signing seems to have been sanctioned by the Caroline Bishops. 'The lawfulness of crossing, not only in Baptism, but in the Supper and anywhere, is avowed.' *A Parallel*, quoted in *Hierurgia*, 378.

36 The remaining prayer of the first part of the Sarum Canon, *Quam Oblationem*, is rendered almost exactly by the clause '*And grant that we receiving*' in our Consecration prayer. There is therefore no need— as there is certainly no authority—for repeating over again the ancient prayers in the pause before the Consecration. (Comp. the P.B. of 1549, where the Prayer for the State of the Church comes after the

Sanctus, and is joined to the Consecration Prayer.) But there has always been a slight pause before the commencement of the Consecration Prayer. See *e.g.* Cookson's *Companion to the Altar* (3rd ed. 1789), where the communicant is given a private meditation of 159 words to fill up the silent pause before the Consecration Prayer.

37 The First Prayer Book ordered the communicants to tarry 'in the choir, or in some convenient place nigh unto the choir,' the rest to depart out of the choir. This custom, it may here be noted, of the non-communicants attending the service from the body of the church was long continued, and has never been forbidden in our service-books. Cf. Robertson, 195-9.

38 The P. B. of 1549 says, 'Then shall this general Confession be made, in the name of all those that are minded to receive the Holy Communion, either by one of them or else by one of the ministers, or by the Priest himself, all kneeling humbly upon their knees.' The Scottish Liturgy of 1637 has 'by the presbyter himself or the deacon, both he and all the people kneeling humbly.' It is clear from these that, in the absence of ministers, the priest may say the Confession himself. The omission of the communicants in the later rubric was very likely due to the practical difficulty in one of them leading.

39 *Lincoln Judgement*, 83-4.

40 The *Benedictus* and *Agnus* have been pronounced lawful by the Lincoln Judgement. It is important that they should always be sung.

41 But a light at the Elevation is very different from a theatrical processional entry of candles.

42 The use of a bell later, as a signal for communicants to approach, is convenient, though without authority.

43 This he may do either by solemnly bowing or by kneeling on one knee. The old *rubrics* are in favour of bowing or bending the body; but the genuflexion seems to have been introduced some time before the Reformation in some places. The Caroline divines used very profound bows. *Hierurgia*, 39, 56.

44 In the Sarum rite these words (which were only said after the Consecration of the chalice) were clearly connected with the actual Elevation, 'Here let him elevate the chalice, saying, "As often as ye shall do these things, ye shall do them in remembrance of Me."' Therefore they should not be said before the Elevation.

45 This is the reason of the knot on the stem of the chalice, for convenience in the holding.

46 The order for the elevation of the Chalice was of considerably later date than that for the elevation of the Host (which was itself as late as the end of the eleventh century). When it was ordered, the rubrics are careful to say that it must not be elevated very high. To this day the conservative order of the Carthusians elevate the Host only. Bridgett, ii. 6.

47 The somewhat minute directions for the Canon taken from foreign sources, seem sometimes to cross our Prayer Book rubrics. It is not advisable to tie ourselves down to Baldeschi, Le Vavasseur, and the *Missale Romanum*.

48 See on this subject, *Notes on Ceremonial* (pp. 183-4); Mr. Lacey on *Liturgical Interpolations* (Alcuin C. tract): Duchesne, *Origines du Culte Chrétien*, pp. 172-3.

49 *St. Cyril's Catech. Lectures*, xxiii.

50 The Prayer Book of 1549 has, 'Then the Priest turning him to the people, shall let them depart with this blessing.' For the reason why this order should be kept and the priest turn *before* giving the blessing (not in the middle of it) see Dr. W. Legg, *S.P.E.S. Trans.* ii. 124.

51 Nothing can be clearer than the directions, first to cover what remains of the Blessed Sacrament with a corporal after the Communion, and secondly to consume it immediately after the Blessing. It seems therefore incredible that some priests should consume what remains before the *Paternoster*, on the ground that our rubrics are obscure.

52 These are the directions of the sixth rubric at the end of our service. It is certainly not directed against the practice of reservation. It was inserted in 1662 to guard against irreverence. A certain class of clergy had carried what remained of the Blessed Sacrament into their own homes and used it for domestic purposes. To prevent this horrible sacrilege the rubric was inserted—'And if any of the Bread and Wine remain unconsecrated, the Curate shall have it to his own use: but if any remain of that which was consecrated, it shall not be carried out of the Church, but the Priest and such other of the Communicants as he shall then call unto him, shall, immediately after the Blessing, reverently eat and drink the same.'

53 See *Lincoln Judgement*, 14-17.

54 The directions of the Missal, Customary, and the Manual of 1554, are at first sight confusing; but a little study removes the difficulty, which is caused by the ablutions being first summarised '*vinum et aquam,*' and then explained separately, as if there were three acts instead of two. The directions here given are the same as those in *Notes on Ceremonial* (99, 128), which seem to be the most correct, as they are certainly the most simple and practical. The pouring of water into the paten was ordered by a Constitution of Archbishop Edmund, 1246.

55 The. cross, or other device, on the foot of the chalice marks the part to be used for communicating.

56 The Last Gospel appeared in the Sarum Missal long before it was in the Roman. It is ordered to be said *in redeundo,* though in small churches where the priest vested and unvested at the altar it was often said at the altar also. Cf. Barnes, *Low Mass in England*, p. 17.

57 When, however, English tradition is silent, it is safer to do a thing in the simplest and most natural way,—not to follow other guides. If, for instance, the deacon is standing in his usual place, it seems better for him, when our books are silent, to remain where he is, and not to move elsewhere.

CHAPTER VII
OTHER SERVICES

HOLY BAPTISM.

The parson is ordered by the first rubric to admonish the people 'that it is most convenient that Baptism should not be administered but upon Sundays, and other Holy-days,' for the excellent reasons that a congregation should be present to testify to the receiving of the newly baptized into the number of Christ's Church, and that those present should be reminded of their profession. But 'if necessity so require' baptism is allowed upon any other day. The time of the Sacrament is fixed for Mattins or Evensong, immediately after the last lesson. By Canon 68 the clergy are bound, under pain of suspension, to christen any child after the last lesson on any Sunday or Holy Day, if the parents (being parishioners) desire it, and give 'convenient warning.'

The desire of the Prayer Book to make much of this holy Sacrament is therefore clear, and is against the modern custom of making the service practically one for the private baptism of children. If the people are ever to be taught the importance of Holy Baptism, the clergy must obey the Prayer Book better.

Solemn Baptism. We will, therefore, first consider a really public service, Solemn Baptism, what has been called a 'choral celebration' of the holy Sacrament of Baptism. For though 'necessity' often does 'require' a week-day evening or Sunday afternoon ministration, yet we are bound to do so in the presence of the congregation at least on some Sundays in the year.[1] Of course sponsors must be arranged with to be present; and the ministration had better be announced in the magazine.

On a Sunday evening, therefore, those who are to be baptized being in church, after the second lesson has been read, the solemn ministration begins.

The priest, wearing a white stole and cope,[2] leaves the chancel with servers and choir, in the following order:—cross; torches; thurifer; two servers, one carrying the book, the other a lighted candle and a napkin (and the shell, if it be used); the priest; the choir (or as many of the choristers as there be room for by the font).[3] A hymn (*e.g.* 325) or antiphon may be sung during the procession. The font 'is then to be filled with pure water,'[4] not a tenth part filled, nor some small vessel only standing in the font,[5] but the font itself is to have an ample measure of water in it.

The priest stands at the font facing east, on his right the server holding the font-candle, on his left the other server with the book (which he had best lay on the font until the benediction and baptizing). In front of the font stands the thurifer, behind him the cross-bearer, both facing the priest; the torch-bearers stand on either side of the cross-bearer facing the same way. Behind the priest the choir is ranged, if there be room, facing east. On the right and left of the font stand the sponsors, kneelers being provided for them and cards of the service.

Having privately inquired of the sponsors if the child be a boy or a girl, should there be only one child, the priest asks them in low but distinct voice (not, of course, on a note) *'Hath this child.'* Then he says in a loud voice, so that all the congregation may hear, *'Dearly beloved'*; then on a note, *'Let us pray,'* and the two next prayers, standing, while the people kneel and sing the *Amens*. The servers and choir do not kneel. Then all stand for the Gospel, before and after which the usual versicles should be sung.[6] The Exhortation is said in a loud voice, all standing. The priest alone says the Thanksgiving, the *Amen* being in italics. In a low but clear voice he addresses the sponsors, and asks the Questions, to which they reply.

Then follows the Blessing of the Font, the form being a condensation of the old *Benedictio Fontis*. Some of the old ritual acts have no longer the words that accompanied them; but the words which were said while the priest held the font-candle in the water[7] have their counterpart in our four short prayers, which are taken from an ancient Gallican rite. Therefore the priest might hold the base of the candle in the water during these short prayers, signing the water with it as he puts it in; at least the candle might be held close to the font for the Benediction. The people stand and sing the *Amens*. Continuing on a note, the priest says the longer prayer, *'Almighty, ever-living God.'* At the words, *'Sanctify this water,'* the priest divides the water with his right hand in the form of a cross,[8] afterwards wiping his fingers with the napkin which the server holds out to him.

The priest then takes the children (their caps having been removed), and baptizes them one by one. If he be inexperienced, he should ask some woman to instruct him in the proper manner of holding babies; it is really important, both for the sake of the parents, and for that of quietness, that he should be handy with children. He takes the child so that its head lies on his left arm; but in the case of an adult he is told to 'take each person to be baptized by the right hand, and placing him conveniently by the Font, according to his discretion, shall ask the Godfathers and Godmothers the Name.' In the case of a big child he had better let the mother hold it 'conveniently by' the font, where it should kneel down; but he must then take its right hand.

Our rubric orders immersion[9] unless the sponsors 'certify that the child is weak,' which they would no doubt generally do in these degenerate days. But it is a pity that immersion has gone so entirely out of practice; and in warm weather, if the sponsors wish it, the child should be dipped (three times according to the First Prayer Book), but 'discreetly and warily.' The water may in this case be slightly warmed. If the child is not dipped, the priest must 'pour' (not sprinkle) water upon it—the best way is to pour it three times over its forehead and head with his right hand.[10] He must be very careful to say the words *during* the pouring of the water. The priest alone says this and the following *Amen*. He then wipes the child's head with the napkin.

The priest then says '*We receive*,' still holding the child, and makes the sign of the cross with his thumb, not using water again.[11] It is a beautiful, significant ancient custom (and one much appreciated) to kiss the child on the forehead before giving it back.

The priest says these words very solemnly, and he should know them by heart. As a precaution the server should hold the book up a little to his right. In most places the book should be taken off the font from before the Benediction till after the Reception, lest it be spotted with water.

When the priest had given the child back to the sponsors he was ordered in the First Prayer Book, in accordance with a very ancient custom, to 'put on him his white vesture, commonly called the Chrisom,' and then to anoint him upon the head. The chrisom was brought back by the mother at her Churching.

If a hymn is sung (*e.g.* 328), this is an appropriate place.

In a loud voice the priest says '*Seeing now*,' and the following *Paternoster* and Thanksgiving on a note, 'all,' *i.e.* the people, kneeling. The people join in the *Paternoster* and sing the *Amen* to the Thanksgiving.

'Then, all standing up, the priest shall say to the Godfathers and Godmothers this Exhortation,' in a lower voice but quite audibly for the congregation; and he may well lay special stress on the things they have to do.

After the last Exhortation, let the choir form up and return to the chancel as they came, singing, if it is desired, a hymn, or Psalm xxxii., as they go: perhaps it might be permissible to sing the *Nunc Dimittis* in this way. Evensong is then proceeded with.

Care must be taken that the filling in of the register be not forgotten on these occasions.

At the less public ministrations, which are often a necessity with us, care should be taken that there is at least one server with a lighted torch. He may also carry the napkin and book; the verger may then fill the font, and hold the book during the Benediction and baptizing. The priest will wear a white stole, but not a cope. Cards of the service should be provided for those assisting; they can be got from the S.P.C.K. Kneelers round the font should also be provided. After the service one of the sponsors or parents should go to the vestry that the register may be carefully filled in.

For private baptism the priest should take a surplice and white stole. A special vessel should be used: this should not be a toy font, but the basin employed for washing the altar-linen (according to Lyndwode), or that used at the Offertory. Some collects from the Public service are ordered by the rubric, if there is time, at the beginning of the Ministration. A deacon may only baptize 'in the absence of the priest.'[12] Children privately baptized should, in the event of their recovery, be afterwards solemnly received in church, in the manner appointed in the office for Private Baptism. At the end of this office there is a form for conditional Baptism.

The rubric for the Baptism of 'Such as are of Riper Years' (not only adults, but all those who are 'able to answer for themselves') orders that they shall be carefully instructed and examined, and 'be exhorted to prepare themselves with Prayers and Fasting for the receiving of this holy Sacrament.' Those of riper years should be baptized by a priest; deacons at their ordination are only given authority to baptize *infants*, in the absence of the priest. This limitation was added at the last revision, when the office for those of Riper Years was also added, and every mention of the word 'minister' carefully excluded. The first rubric at the end of this service recommends that Confirmation follow speedily. The second allows the substitution of the words 'Child' or 'Person' for 'Infant.' Those of riper years answer the Questions themselves. It is seemly for them to kneel down to receive the sacrament of baptism; and there is no. need for the water to return into the font,—indeed in the old office immediately after its benediction some of the water was thrown out of the font into the four parts of the church.[13] The priest is directed by our rubric only to take him by the right hand and place him 'conveniently by the font, according to his discretion,' and then to ask the sponsors his name, and then to 'dip him in the water, or pour water upon him.' It is best that the person to be baptized should have a towel over his shoulders; indeed, it is necessary if the water is properly 'poured.'

There is no authority with us for the use of a second stole of another colour. It would be difficult also to find one for the use of a shell or other vessel for pouring the water; though this latter practice may be defended on utilitarian grounds. But the convenience in pouring is not secured by the shallow shells that are sometimes sold: a silver or pewter vessel of some capacity should be used, or else a deep shell, if anything of the kind is used at all. The font should be emptied directly after a baptism.

THE CATECHISM.

The rubric directs that the Curate shall 'diligently upon Sundays and Holy-days, after the second Lesson at Evening Prayer, openly in the church instruct and examine' some children 'in some part of this Catechism.' Canon 59 not only insists upon this catechism on Sundays and Holy-days, and orders parents and masters to send those in their charge, but also orders the Bishop to inflict excommunication, for a third offence, on any Minister that neglects his duty herein. The duration of the Catechism is fixed by the Canon at 'half an hour or more'; the time (though in this it is over-ridden by the rubric) at '*before* Evening Prayer.'

It is a pity that this rubric should have fallen into such abeyance. It is true that the use of gas, and other modern customs, have put Evensong so late that it is sometimes inconvenient to take the children during the service. But in the country it would be thought that the parson would often do more good by catechising before his people than by exhausting his powers in a second sermon. 'He that preacheth twice a day prateth at least once,' said Bishop Andrewes.

At least the spirit of the rubric can always be obeyed. 1. There should be a Catechism every Sunday. 2. The children must be brought to church on the Holy-days as well, and there instructed. There is no excuse for ignoring the Holy-days, and bringing our children up to disregard them. 3. The catechetical method is to be observed; they are to be examined as well as instructed. 4. The Church Catechism is to be the text of all instruction, its sacramental doctrine as well as the rest. Lastly, cannot this be done sometimes, at least, openly in church, at Evening Prayer ? The clergy do not try. If they did they would find that a quite short catechism would interest the people enormously, teach them much that they do not know, and be a great pride and delight to the children.

There is one word more to be said. The curate is to catechise 'diligently,' in the best possible way. The ancient tradition of catechising has been unfortunately lost in this country, and its revival has been very largely on the 'shortened Evensong' lines, with the Collect about babes and sucklings (as if we were determined to drive away the older children). This is neither liturgically correct nor practically convenient.

Now, the tradition was never lost in France; and, if the parson reads the works of Dupanloup and the adaptations of the Method of St. Sulpice by Mr. Spencer Jones, he will, I am sure, feel that the 'diligence' of his methods needs improving. Let me therefore here reproduce Mr. Spencer Jones's outline of an afternoon Catechism[14]:—Opening prayer (one collect, at chancel step, all standing). Hymn. The Questioning (in pulpit). Hymn (during which the Little Catechism, the infants, file out). Office (catechist standing half-way down middle alley: 1. Creed. 2. One short Prayer for the Catechism. 3. Collect for the day. 4. Lord's Prayer). Report on Analyses (from chancel step). Hymn. The Instruction (in pulpit; and sometimes an Admonition). Hymn (two verses). Reading of the Gospel, and a short Homily thereon (in pulpit). Hymn. Last Prayers (catechist standing in alley: one collect and the Grace). Departure (by classes; head catechist in pulpit, assistant catechist at the door). The whole to last one hour.

It will be noticed that the characteristics of this method are frequent changes, and shortness of prayers, which are absolutely necessary if the service and the prayers are to be real to the children; that the catechist stands in the most convenient, instead of the most inconvenient, places for his work, and gives point and interest to the various parts by the significant changes of his position; that the exercises are very varied and distinct; that the children take a very definite part, even to the writing of little analyses or compositions; that there is no ceremonial, the catechists wearing only their surplices, and there being no one in the chancel.

On the festivals of the Catechism, which are usually on the Sunday after each quarter day, small prizes are given; and ceremonial and processions (in which all the children take part) may be used.

The Prayer Book knows nothing of Sunday-schools, which became a necessity owing to the want of 'diligence' on the part of the clergy. A feature of the method I have sketched is that, instead of the Catechism being a wind-up to the Sunday-school, the school is merely an introduction to the Catechism. One lesson of our rubric is that the main part of the teaching should be given by the clergy, whose duty it is to become experts in catechising, and not by teachers who in the nature of things are not generally experts.

On Holy-days, according to the Rubric, the children should be instructed in church; and the only practicable time in many places is before their day-school begins. This way of keeping the red-letter days is invaluable; and as such services are a solemn commemoration of the day, in some places they might be more on liturgical lines. Apart from the question whether those who are unconfirmed ought to be taken to the Holy Mysteries, there is hardly time for a children's Eucharist, if the rubric is obeyed as to instruction. And in these days, surely, instruction in the first place is all-important. A service on the following lines has been found to work very well:— Our Father, to end of *Venite*, and Lesson (for the day, or Gospel). *Benedictus*. Creed to end of third collect. Hymn. A short Catechism on the subject for the day. Hymn. Prayer of St. Chrysostom, and Grace. If incense is used at the *Benedictus*, the priest remaining in his cope and standing before the altar on the pavement till the hymn before catechising begins, a sufficiently solemn character is given to the service. It is difficult for a large congregation of children to find out special psalms, and the *Te Deum* is perhaps rather long for them. If the Instruction lasts within a quarter of an hour, such a service will be over in half an hour.

THE SOLEMNISATION OF MATRIMONY.

Deacons should not solemnise a marriage; for although such a marriage is perfectly valid (the blessing not being an essential part of the rite), yet it is very undesirable, as well as irregular, that marriage should be solemnised without the nuptial blessing.

The 'Curate' must have, besides his own register, a 'Certificate of the Banns being thrice asked from the other Parish.' Certificate books should be kept for this purpose. Marriage by licence should be discouraged, except under special circumstances.

The Solemnisation should, if possible, be immediately followed by the Holy Communion, at which the couple should communicate. 'It is convenient [*i.e.* proper][15] that the newly married persons should receive the holy Communion at the time of their Marriage, or at the first opportunity after their Marriage.' This would fix the service early in the day, whence the use of the term Wedding *Breakfast*. In any case afternoon marriages should be discouraged. Marriage should also be discouraged 'in the Lent, or other time prohibited.' These times set down in Almanacks as late as the last century are given in Dr. Legg's Calendar: they are not the same as those now set forth at Rome.

Before the service, the candles are lit, and two cushions laid on the sanctuary step for the couple.

If the service is choral, the priest may wear a cope as well as his white stole (over his albe, etc., if there is to be a Nuptial Mass). On occasions of this kind it is important that the pomp should not be all on the secular side. The priest (holding the book, in which is a slip of paper with the Christian names), with the assistant clergy (who do not wear stoles) in front of him, preceded by verger, cross, torches, and perhaps a boy carrying the book close to him, and followed by the choir, should go to meet the bride and her attendants, and return with them following while a hymn is sung. The distinction between prayers, public addresses, and the personal addresses ('speaking unto the persons that shall be married') should be observed, as in Baptism.

The 'friends and neighbours' being seated, the bridegroom, who has taken up his position with the best-man before the bride came up, stands on the right and the bride on his left, in 'the body of the church,' near the chancel gates being the most convenient. They had better now take off their gloves. The priest stands facing them with his back to the chancel, and the torchbearers hold their torches on either side. The verger stands near him, and the cross is rested on the ground behind the priest. The best-man stands at the side of the bridegroom, and the 'father or friend' of the woman at that of the bride, both a little behind: the mother often wishes also to be near the bride; and the bridesmaids may stand behind the group.

After the Betrothal comes the Giving Away. The priest is directed to receive the woman 'at her father's or friend's hands,' and then 'cause the Man with his right hand to take the Woman by her right hand,' which he will best do by taking her hand from that of the father and placing it in that of the bridegroom. Still holding her hand, the bridegroom says the words after the priest, who should divide them into very short sentences. The priest generally has to whisper 'loose hands,' and to see that the woman takes the man's right hand with her right hand. After she has said the words after the priest, he may have to tell them again to loose hands.

The best-man has meanwhile got the ring ready; this he hands to the bridegroom together with the fees, who lays both upon the book, which the priest holds out to him open. There is no reason why the 'accustomed duty'[16] (substituted for the 'spousal money' of the First Prayer Book) should not be placed on the book with the ring, as our rubric directs. The priest hands the fees to the verger, who receives them in a plate or bag.

The priest then gives the ring to the bridegroom, who at once puts it on 'the fourth finger of the woman's left hand,' and holds it there while he says, in short sentences after the priest ('taught by the priest'), 'With this ring.' They then loose hands and 'both kneel down' (the rest all remaining standing), while the priest says 'Let us pray' and the prayer. He then stoops down, and joining 'their right hands together'[17] says 'Those whom.'

At the Blessing 'God the Father' (as well as at the final Blessing 'Almighty God, who') the priest makes the sign of the cross according to the First Prayer Book.

One of the two Psalms is then sung in procession to the altar, the priest and servers first; the married couple (and no one else of the party) follow them, being directed what to do by the verger. The priest does not turn round till the conclusion of the Gloria.

At the conclusion of the Gloria, the bride and bridegroom kneel 'before the Lord's Table,' on the step of the sanctuary. The priest, 'standing at the Table,' on the foot-pace, 'and turning his face towards them,' begins the Kyries. All sing the responses, and join in the Lord's Prayer. The priest remains facing west to the end, and the couple continue to kneel.

The priest is at liberty (indeed he is expected by the rubric) to substitute a sermon—which may be a very short nuptial address—for the Exhortation. If there is to be a nuptial Mass, the Sermon or Exhortation will be delivered after the Creed.

If two priests take the service, they should not chop it about; but one should take the first part of the service, and the other should go to the altar for the last part, the first priest standing at one side in the sanctuary, and facing across it. A third priest may give the final exhortation.

THE VISITATION OF THE SICK.

This beautiful service is not used or known enough by the clergy. Nearly all its prayers and rubrics are to be found in the ancient manuals of the Church of England, and some of the prayers can be traced to almost primitive times. It is a solemn rite; and does not seem to be intended for use more than once in an illness. Even when it is not advisable to use it in full, the short prayers will still be found invaluable; and those who visit the sick should know the service well.

In this service, too, is given the English Church's form of Absolution after private Confession.

In the office for the Communion of the Sick is a special Collect, and very short Epistle and Gospel. The priest is told by the rubric to begin the service here, and then to proceed at once to 'Ye that do truly.' He should be very careful not to confuse the sick man by any unfamiliar ritual actions.

The eucharistic vestments should be worn, if possible, for the Communion, but as it is often not practicable or advisable to wear them, the surplice and stole are frequently used instead. The surplice should be worn for the Visitation, and a stole may (not must) be worn for the Absolution. When the chasuble, etc., are used, a special set of linen vestments should be kept apart for sick communion. In many cases it will be found convenient to keep a plain stole in the vestry for taking out to people's houses. For the Communion a table should be got ready in the room and covered with a clean white cloth; on it should stand a crucifix or cross and two lighted candles, or at the least one candle without a cross. Care should be taken to consecrate only as much as is absolutely necessary. Ancient authority allows of any that remains being consumed in the fire if it is impossible for the sick man or the priest to consume it. This applies equally to the ablutions, which may be consumed by the sick person.

It is sometimes absolutely necessary to take the Sacrament out of church to a sick person's house, either because of infection, or because of extremity, or because the patient cannot bear the time needed for a celebration; often five minutes is as long as a sick man can endure. The priest will then wear a stole (and if the distance be not far a surplice also),[18] and will carry the pyx, veiled, with the cord of the purse round his neck. He should wear a cloak to cover all; and if a server can walk before him with a lantern it is better. The practice of dipping the Species of bread into the Chalice has authority against it.

A table should be prepared with a clean cloth, at least one candle, and the cruets for the ablutions. On arriving at the house the priest should say 'Peace be' as in the Visitation. He lays the pyx upon the linen cloth; and then should be said at least (if it be possible) the Confession, Absolution, Words of Administration, Prayer of Thanksgiving, Blessing.

In all cases of sick communion it is best for some one who knows the people to go to the house a quarter of an hour before with the vessels, bread, water, wine, linen, and candlesticks, and have everything ready for the priest as if it were in church. It is often very distressing to the sick person if there is a scramble to get things straight when the priest has arrived. When all is in order, there will be a few minutes' quiet time of prayer and preparation before the priest comes.

The following precautions should be observed with infectious cases: —

Avoid visiting dangerous cases of illness with the stomach in an empty condition, or with the lungs exhausted by a quick ascent of stairs. Calmness is a great safeguard. So is a biscuit and a glass of wine.

In infectious cases, therefore, it is obvious that communion except with the reserved Sacrament is dangerous.

In all infectious cases the sick person should consume all that remains of the species of wine, and should also, in accordance with the wise ancient practice, consume the ablutions. When he cannot, then any that remains of the Sacrament and also the ablutions should be burnt on the fire. Indeed, in all sickness, whether infection is declared or not, the sick person should be communicated last, as the rubric directs, and no one should touch the chalice after him.

In case of typhoid and all throat diseases communion with the chalice is unsafe. Care is especially necessary, as diphtheria is sometimes called by a milder name, and there are also certain virulently infectious diseases about which professional etiquette among doctors enjoins silence. If a chalice is used (and a glass one is best for this purpose) it should be washed at once inside and out with water; and then taken home and washed in a solution of 1 in 20 of carbolic acid. It is best, however, to use a cheap spoon, and to put it at once in the fire.

The cassock is an ideal protective garment from the medical point of view, but it must be of silk or other close material. Immediately on leaving the patient it should be taken off, given a good shake, and hung in the air for six hours; and the parson should air his clothes by a short walk. Indeed, he should never enter his own, or any other house, until he has aired his person by a walk.

In cases of virulent infection (such as small-pox, typhus, or scarlet-fever in the peeling stage), the cassock as well as the surplice should be washed; and, if a stole is used, it should be of linen, so that it too can be washed.

Silk vestments should never be used for sick communions. The vestments should be of linen, and always washed after use. As violet is the colour for the Visitation and Communion of the Sick, blue linen would be a good material.

The priest should never place himself between an infectious patient and the fire; for the air will then be drawn over his person.

He should not inhale the breath of the patient.

He should not keep his hand in contact with that of the patient.

He should wash his hands at once in a solution of corrosive sublimate, having first removed any gold or silver rings. Soloids of the sublimate, manufactured by Burroughs and Welcome, can be got at any chemist's; one soloid is to be dissolved in a pint of water. If the patient has coughed any matter on to the priest's face, he should also wash his face in the solution.

He should never eat any food in an infectious house.

When he is much among infectious cases, as during an epidemic, he should take a hot bath every night,. and a Turkish bath once a week.

These precautions are necessary, not only for his own sake, but for that also of his other parishioners.

THE BURIAL OF THE DEAD.

In nothing is reform more needed than in the manner of conducting funerals. The unutterably horrible customs of fifty years ago are not yet by any means extinct; and the more decent modifications of them still leave very much to be desired.

One principle which will, I think, commend itself to all who live among the poor, as well as to those who live among the rich, is the reduction of secular pomp.

To secure this another principle is needed, the increase of sacred pomp. Something there must be at these sad occasions; and, if the Church does not supply what the mourners crave for, the world will step in with the miserable trappings of its pride. It must be within the experience of every parson that even those who dislike 'ritual' on other occasions are most grateful for its comfort at this time, when comfort is so much needed.

But the Church's pomp should not be copied from that of the world, as now happens abroad, where the undertakers are allowed practically to take over the church for the day.

Black is the liturgical colour for these occasions. But this does not mean that the church should be given up to the trappings of undertakers. The vestments should be black (except for a child under seven years of age, when white should be used); though there were many exceptions to this,[19] blue copes were common, and violet (i.e. dark blue) was regarded as a form of black. But the church itself should be left as usual, only the frontal being changed to black or violet; and the pall, as we have seen, may be of many colours. Apparels, too, need not be changed, so long as they go with the vestments.

The passing bell should always be rung before and not after death; the reason of this ancient custom being that the faithful may pray for the dying person. Canon 6 orders:—'When any is passing out of this life a bell shall be tolled, and the minister shall not then slack to do his last duty. And after the party's death (if so it fall out), there shall be rung no more but one short peal and one other before the burial and one other after the burial.'

Therefore the custom of tolling the bell for any length of time before the funeral is not authorised. It would seem best only to toll it from the time the funeral procession nears the churchyard gate until it enters the porch. A handbell may well be rung before the funeral procession, in accordance with ancient custom, from the moment it leaves the house. A pall should always be used, and the coffin never be carried through the streets, or into church, uncovered. The pall should be the property of the church and not of the undertaker. The excessive use of flowers is to be deprecated.

In church all will be ready; the altar candles lit (whether there is to be a Mass or not), and the funeral candlesticks standing in their place before the chancel steps. Incense should, if possible, always be used at funerals. The clerk will have the funeral cross ready if there be one; if not, then the Lenten cross, or the ordinary processional cross if there be but one. The torchbearers will use their ordinary torches, unless they have lanterns, which are more convenient for out-door processions.

At the first stroke of the bell, the procession will leave the church, so as to arrive at the gate of the churchyard as the funeral procession enters. It will go in the usual order (cross, torches, thurifer, sacred ministers, priest, choir). If there is to be a Celebration of the Holy Communion, the priest will wear a black cope over his albe, etc., and the rest their proper vestments (including dalmatics and tunicles); if not, the priest need not wear a stole over his surplice, but he may well wear a cope or a choral-cope. All should wear square caps; but during any *prayers* all heads should be uncovered, or covered only with a coif. The academical hood does not make a good head-dress. The mourners and choir may all carry torches if it be desired.

'The Priest and Clerks meeting the Corpse at the entrance of the Church-yard, and going before it, either into the Church, or towards the Grave, shall say, or sing,' the opening Sentences. The rubric does not sanction the priest meeting the Corpse only at the church-door;[20] but it does allow of the corpse not being taken into the church at all, apparently if sanitary reasons make this necessary. The order of the procession should be servers, priest, choir, the coffin, the mourners following behind.

'After they are come into the Church, shall be read one or both of these Psalms following.' It would seem, therefore, that the Psalm or Psalms should be commenced as soon as the procession has entered the church: this is certainly more convenient and less gloomy than for the procession to go up the alley in silence.

The choir will go straight into the chancel, and the clerk will put down his cross against the sanctuary wall. The coffin will be laid on the bier outside the chancel-gates between the candles, its feet to the east, the bearers going to the side. The priest or minister will read the lesson from the choir.

If there is to be a Eucharist, which is most desirable, the celebrant may prepare himself while the Lesson is being read. The Lesson should be read just as it stands, *sine titulo* and *sine conclusione*.

Collects, Epistles, and Gospels can be found in Canon Carter's book. For infants, the collect, epistle, and gospel for Michaelmas should be used. The Introit in the First Prayer Book was Ps. 42, *Quemadmodum* (not omitting the *Gloria*). The *Dies Irae* (A. and M. 393) was sometimes sung as a Sequence before the Gospel. Incense should be used; and the coffin censed during the Introit, during the Gradual, and after the censing at the Offertory.

At the end of the Eucharist, or of the Lesson if there be no Eucharist, the procession goes to the grave, in the same order and vestments as before. A hymn may be sung as the procession goes (e.g. 399).

It seems generally most convenient[21] for the cross-bearer to stand at the foot of the grave, looking west, and the priest to stand at the head looking east. The torchbearers holding their torches on either side of the priest's book, the thurifer standing near the grave, the choir and the mourners grouping themselves as may be most convenient.

'While the corpse is made ready to be laid into the earth, the Priest shall say, or the Priest and Clerks shall sing,' the Anthem, '*Man that is born.*' It is clear from the next rubric that the body must also be lowered into the grave during this Anthem: the men must therefore be taught not to wait till the Anthem is finished as they sometimes do.

As soon as the Anthem is finished, 'then, while the earth shall be cast upon the Body by some standing by [not by the priest], the Priest shall say the Commendation.' Anciently the earth was strewn in the form of a cross. It is still the custom to cast it in thrice.

Then follows the singing or saying of the second Anthem. All join in the *Paternoster*, and might sign themselves at the Grace. Another hymn, or one of the Penitential Psalms, might be sung in returning. At the burial of an infant, Ps. 113 (*Laudate pueri*), or Ps. 148 (*Laudate Dominum*) may be sung.

In towns, where there is no churchyard, and the interment has to be in a distant cemetery, the first part of the service should still, if possible, be said in the parish church. The bearers will then remove the coffin at the conclusion of the Eucharist, or of the Lesson if there be no Eucharist.

Monuments. There are few churchyards that have not been spoiled by ill-chosen monuments. In the Middle Ages (when, by the way, the dead were infinitely better remembered than at the present day), there were few monuments in the churchyard, and those generally of a simple kind such as a wooden cross with a plain weathering. In more recent times appeared plain head-stones, and also monuments of great ugliness and pretension. It may be questioned, however, whether even in the worst period of Georgian paganism, the appearance of our churchyards was half as bad as the ostentation of the last thirty years has made it.

This is. mainly due to the fact that people will not be contented with the use of ordinary stone, but desire memorials of marble and granite. Now, polished granite is bad enough as a rule; but marble is far worse. It is utterly out of character with its surroundings, and stands out in glaring consequence, refusing to blend with the quiet grey stone of the church behind it. As it is nearly always ill-proportioned, clumsy, and badly lettered, this wretched prominence is the more unfortunate; and in our climate, marble becomes more harsh and dismal in colour every year. A modern churchyard gives the most wretched impression of competitive self-advertisement; and is, I venture to think, in spite of the obtrusive use of the cross in our monuments, quite as out of harmony with the Christian spirit as were the quiet headstones and occasional square enormities of our grandfathers.

Nearly every old church, and every cathedral, is being ruined by the garish setting of white monuments that is creeping round it. In addition to this, our cathedrals are being spoilt within by the practice of putting up a 'recumbent effigy' to every prelate that dies—so important do we moderns fancy ourselves. It is high time that the clergy taught a more humble spirit, and that monuments were used far more seldom both within and without our churches. There is now and then good cause for them; but respectability and death are not in themselves sufficient reason for a prominent *siste viator*.

Much the best memorial is something of real use or beauty for the church. Yet even in such cases one often cannot but notice with pain how loudly some voice of brass advertises the family of the deceased.

Brasses need not be hideous; but almost all modern ones are. A very great deal can be done with incised brass, and far more if it is treated with coloured enamels, by a real artist.[22] Tombstones, tablets, and memorials of all kinds should not be articles of commerce.

It is worth while remembering that the Court of Arches decided (in the case of Woolfrey *v.* Breeks) that the Incumbent had no power to exclude an incription because it contained the petition, 'Pray for the soul of J. Woolfrey. It is a holy and wholesome thought to pray for the dead.' The Court declared that the inscription 'was not illegal, as by no canon or authority of the Church in these realms had the practice of praying for the dead been expressly prohibited.'

THE CHURCHING OF WOMEN.

The woman to be churched shall come into the church 'decently apparelled.' This at least as late as Charles II.'s reign meant that she was to wear the white veil, which was certified by the bishops a little earlier to be 'according to the ancient usage of the Church of England.'[23]

She is to 'kneel down in some convenient place, as hath been accustomed, or as the Ordinary shall direct.' The most accustomed place is outside the chancel-gates, at a desk or on the steps: in the Prayer Book of 1552 it is 'nigh unto the place where the Table standeth'; in that of 1549 it is 'nigh unto the quire door'; in both it is 'a convenient place.'

'Standing by her' is the position of the priest in the First Prayer Book. He should stand in front of her, facing west, throughout the service.

He should wear the vestments of whatever service is to follow,[24] and be accompanied by the clerk, or verger, to lead the responses. White is the colour for Churching.

The best time for Churching is just before a Celebration, 'and, if there be a Communion, it is convenient that she receive the holy Communion.' On these occasions the first Psalm is the more appropriate.

By the bishops of the sixteenth and seventeenth centuries penance was first required in the case of an unmarried woman; and the anglican divines at the Savoy Conference declared that 'she is to do penance before she is churched.'

At the end of the service the woman 'must offer accustomed offerings.' The priest had better have a plate by him for this purpose. The offerings are for the priest himself, like the 'accustomed duty' at weddings.

The second Psalm should not be used if the woman has lost her child.

PROCESSIONS.

The procession is a distinct, significant act of worship: it is not an aimless walk round the church; but it has a definite object, such as the Rood, the Lord's Table, or the Font.

A procession is not the triumphant entry and exit of the choir, nor is any such thing known to the Church as a 'recessional.' Properly, the choir should go quietly to their places when they arrive, and occupy the time before the service with prayer and recollectedness in their stalls, instead of with chatting in the vestry. If, however, they go in all together in processional order, no hymn should be sung, nor should there be any special hymn to accompany their return; and, above all, no cross should be carried. They should be well settled in their places before the ministers enter.

The common forgetfulness of the real meaning of the procession is much to be regretted. A study of the Bible and of Christian usages would correct it. There are three great processions mentioned in the Bible as well as other lesser ones,—the Encircling of Jericho (Josh. vi.), the bringing of the Ark into Jerusalem by David (2 Sam. vi.) to the accompaniment of the 105th Psalm and instrumental music, and the Procession of Palms (Matt. xxi.).[25]

In the Christian Church the earliest form of Procession was the singing of Litanies, with stations or stopping-places for special prayers. This feature is preserved in our Litany, the meaning of which can only be fully brought out if it is sung in procession and stations made for the prayers.

There were always three distinct processions in connection with the Eucharist in the English Church. (1) The solemn procession before the service, not from the vestry, but from the choir back to the altar. (2) The little procession—a very ancient ceremony—when the clerk carried in the sacred vessels. (3) The procession to the rood-loft or to the chancel-gates, for the Gospel. These are treated of in the chapter on the Holy Eucharist.

There were also many special processions, as that to the font, on Easter Eve.

Although there may be a procession every Sunday before the Eucharist, it is more convenient and more in accordance with ancient custom to reserve the procession after Evensong to the red-letter days.

In the Prayer Book there are two processions described, that to the altar in the Marriage Service, and that at a funeral, which is often mutilated in defiance of the rubric. Both these are true processions, full of significance and solemnity: one is the solemn conducting of the couple to the altar, there to be blessed and houselled; the other is the solemn carrying up of the dead body to receive the last blessing and prayers of the Church.

By official custom the 24th Psalm is also sung in procession at the Consecration of Churches. And the old out-door processions at Rogation-tide have also been maintained.

There is only one order in the English Church for processions; and that is for the ministers to walk at the head. When the proper station is made before the Rood, the practical convenience of this, as well as its beauty, is. obvious. The ancient order, which, however it may be modified, we have no right whatever to distort, was as follows:[26]— The vergers, with their wands, making way for the procession, the boy with holy water (in surplice), the 'accolitus' or clerk carrying the cross, the two torchbearers, the thurifer, the sub-deacon, the deacon, the celebrant, the boys of the choir, the men of the choir, other clergy. The boat-bearer's place will be next the thurifer; a boy may also walk in front of the sub-deacon carrying a book for the station-prayers. If there are rulers they should walk between the boys and men of the choir. The bishop will walk last of all, unless he is to officiate, when he will walk in the celebrant's place.

In small churches the procession will always start from the chancel-gates, and go by the south alley, returning up the middle alley, except on penitential occasions, when it will go by the north alley. But in churches that have choir aisles the procession before Mass on great days should go out by the west gates of the choir, and then round by the north choir aisle, behind the high altar (or in front if necessary), and by the south choir aisle to the south aisle, returning as usual. On other occasions in such churches the procession should leave the choir by the north door of the presbytery, and then round by the south aisle as usual.

The use of wind instruments is always a help, and in out-door processions is almost a necessity.[27]

Banners are not a necessity for processions, though they may be an improvement if they are beautiful and not too numerous. A procession in a small church is apt to be top-heavy if there are too many banners. There may be a banner of the patron saint in every church.

If the church has only a middle alley, indoor processions seem out of place.

The thurifer should swing his censer in a simple manner backwards and forwards with short swings, and not attempt any gymnastics. The censer should not be replenished during the procession; nor will it need replenishing if natural incense be used. There are no authoritative directions for the officiant to hold his hands in any particular manner; he should hold them naturally and not affect stained-glass attitudes; but he will not walk well unless he joins them. He should not stare about him. Choir-men often roll about in an ungainly fashion which would not be tolerated for an instant at a military parade. The way to avoid this is to train everybody to take steps no longer than the length of their feet. The choir will also need some drilling before they learn to keep their distances: each person should walk as far from his neighbour as the width of the alley will allow; and each pair should rigidly keep a distance of three to four feet between themselves and the pair in front. The procession must be carefully timed by the verger (who will need a small hymn-book for this) so that the last verse of the hymn has still to be sung when he reaches the chancel-steps.

The processions at the Lord's Supper and Evensong are further described in their place, as are also those for the Litany, etc.

SERMONS.

The time ordered for the Sermon[28] in the Prayer Book is after the Creed at the Eucharist. Those, therefore, who place the morning Sermon at Mattins instead of at the Communion, disobey the Prayer Book, and dislodge the Eucharist from its position as the most public service.

The Prayer Book orders Catechising, and not a Sermon, for Evensong: it may well be asked whether this would not be the wisest course in an age when there is too much loose talking in the pulpit, and too little definite teaching.

Just as the celebrant at the Holy Eucharist keeps on his vestments (with the exception of the chasuble and maniple) for convenience, so at Evensong, for the same reason, the preacher or catechist may retain his surplice, hood, and tippet.[29] The First Prayer Book says that it is 'seemly that graduates, when they do preach, shall use such hoods as pertaineth to their several degrees.' Canon 58, referring to surplices, and Canon 74, referring to gowns, both order graduates to wear their hoods, which at that time is known to have included the use of the tippet or scarf; therefore Canon 58, while forbidding non-graduates to wear a hood, allows them to retain the other part of the clerical dress, the tippet ('so it be not silk'), and to wear it upon their surplices, instead of hoods; while Canon 74 orders both hood and silk tippet for Masters of Arts.

But if lectures are given from the pulpit, or mission addresses, or other unliturgical discourses, the speaker should certainly not wear any special vestments, but only the cassock and gown (with hood and silk tippet, if he have a Master's degree), which is the ordinary canonical dress of the clergy. This is not only the correct course to adopt, but is also often a help in winning those who are unused to other garments; and nothing is more graceful or more convenient for this kind of speaking than a black gown. The Evangelical clergy are now showing the same dislike to preaching in the gown which the Ritualistic clergy showed a generation ago. It is difficult to understand why. The gown is quite as legitimate, and quite as Catholic, as the surplice, even for the canonical sermon, and rather more ritualistic. The preacher, or lecturer, may wear the gown of his degree, or the 'preacher's' gown, which latter, by the way, has nothing to do with Geneva, and being a special priestly gown is more sacerdotal than either the university gown or the surplice. The Genevan party abhorred it 'little, if at all, less than the surplice itself.'[30]

To put it shortly. The preacher at the Lord's Supper, if he is one of the ministers, will lay aside his outer vestment and maniple. But if he is not one of the ministers, and also at Evening Prayer, and at a Marriage when there is no Mass, he may wear either surplice or gown. At other occasions he should wear a gown.

The preacher should on no account wear a stole over his surplice. This practice, which takes away all meaning from the use of the stole, has no authority, ancient or modern. It has been ignorantly copied from Rome, where its use is far from general, being only permitted and not enjoined.

It is convenient and seemly that the verger, in accordance with ancient custom, should conduct the preacher to the pulpit, whenever there is a sermon. The verger goes, verge in hand, up the chancel-steps, to the preacher's stall, and stands before him till the latter follows him; the verger then leads the way to the pulpit, stands aside for the preacher to mount the stairs, and closes the door behind him.

There is no authority for introducing the sermon with a collect or the invocation. The 55th Canon, following a very ancient pre-Reformation custom,[31] orders a Bidding Prayer to be said 'before all Sermons, Lectures, and Homilies.'

The magnificent Bidding Prayer given by the Canon is as follows, but it may be altered or shortened ('in this form, or to this effect, as briefly as conveniently they may'):—

'Ye shall pray for Christ's holy Catholic Church, that is, for the whole congregation of Christian people dispersed throughout the whole world, and especially for the Churches of England, Scotland, and Ireland: and herein I require you most especially to pray for the [King's] most excellent Majesty, our Sovereign Lord [James, King] of England, Scotland, [France] and Ireland, Defender of the Faith, and Supreme Governor in these his realms, and all other his dominions and countries, over all persons in all causes, as well Ecclesiastical as Temporal: ye shall also pray for our gracious Queen [Anne], the noble Prince [Henry], and the rest of the King and Queen's royal issue: ye shall also pray for the Ministers of God's Holy Work and Sacraments, as well Archbishops and Bishops, as other Pastors and Curates; ye shall also pray for the King's most honourable Council, and for all the Nobility and Magistrates of the realm; that all and every of these, in their several callings, may serve truly and painfully to the glory of God, and the edifying and well governing of his people, remembering the account that they must make: also ye shall pray for the whole Commons of this realm, that they may live in the true faith and fear of God, in humble obedience to the King, and brotherly charity one to another. Finally, let us praise God for all those who are departed out of this life in the faith of Christ, and pray unto God that we may have grace to direct our lives after their good example; that, this life ended, we may be made partakers with them of the glorious resurrection in the life everlasting; always concluding with the Lord's Prayer.'

It is an immense pity that this beautiful form of intercession is now so little used. Were it forbidden us, instead of enjoined, it would doubtless be said from half the pulpits in London, instead of being almost confined to the Universities. The only objection to its use that can possibly be raised is that to repeat the Lord's Prayer with a special intention is a Catholic practice.[32] It will be noticed that the essential part is the Lord's Prayer, and that the rest may be modified. Some of the earlier phrases are a little too courtly to be real to modern ears;[33] but the bulk of it should be used at the morning sermon. And at sermons at other times, at least the Lord's Prayer should be said, with a short form of Bidding (such as, *e.g.*, 'Ye shall pray for Christ's Holy Catholic Church and for this Realm'). For afternoon lectures, the Bidding Prayer with a hymn forms a most fitting short service. The people should stand for the Bidding and kneel for the Lord's Prayer.

It has become customary, I know not on what authority, to conclude the sermon with an ascription. The use of a *prayer* at the end of the sermon rests on a custom as old as Cranmer's time.[34] In either case it is better to say the form in the natural voice, and without turning to the east. A painful impression of unreality is sometimes produced by the preacher suddenly wheeling round, and taking a note, at the end of an earnest discourse. It is far more impressive if the Amen also be said by the people quietly and in their natural voice. The introduction of semi-musical habits into the pulpit is altogether to be deprecated. Some preachers let a trace of intonation run through their sermons, and the effect I have seen described as that of a 'dismal howl.' When words are sung they should be sung in tune, but when they are said they should be said with a proper and natural elocution.

Notes

1 The Prayer Book of 1549 has, 'It appeareth by ancient writers that the Sacrament of Baptism in the old time was not commonly ministered but at two times in the year, at Easter and Whitsuntide...Which custom...although it cannot for many considerations be well restored again, yet it is thought good to follow the same as near as conveniently may be.'

2 We read in the 'Cheque-Book' of the Chapel Royal (1605), 'whome the said Arch Bishop baptized with great reverence (being still in his rich cope) who was assisted in the administracion of the Sacrament by the Deane of the Chappell (he allso beinge in his cope).'

3 *Processionale*, 84. At the blessing of the font on Easter Eve, two deacons walked before the priest and ministers, carrying the oil and chrism.

4 The filling of the font, it seems, is part of the ritual of the service, and should be done now, and not before. See Perry, *Purchas J.*, on meaning of the word 'then.'

5 Many bishops, from Parker downwards, enjoin 'that no pots, pails, or basons be used in it or instead of it,'—such having been a favourite practice of the Puritans.—Robertson, 217.

6 It must have been the English custom; for Cosin inserted the '*Glory be*' and the '*Thanks be*' in his own revised Prayer Book; and in some of the ancient offices the *Gloria* was inserted, while it was left, as in our own, to tradition.

7 This ceremony is at least as old as the sixth century.—Blunt, 209.

8 '*Hic dividat aquam manu suo,*' etc. The First Prayer Book prints the sign of the cross after '*sanctify.*' St. Augustine, a godly and ancient Father, twice alludes to the practice of signing the water. It was sanctified as early as the time of Tertullian, who died c. 245. (Blunt, 209, 225.)

9 For immersion there should be provided a very loose woollen garment. Immediately after the immersion the child should be dried

and wrapped in flannel, or else dressed in its clothes, while a hymn is being sung.

10 Bp. Montagu used to require the ancient threefold washing, and other divines favoured it. Even if we overlook its symbolical reference to the three Persons of the Trinity, it is a most needful safeguard to ensure the water actually touching the skin of the person, especially in the case of those with much hair. See also *Church Law*, 49.

11 It has been questioned whether the unction ought not now to be used at *we receive*; as our Church never intended to abolish customs which were used by the ancient Fathers, and unction at Baptism was used in the time of Tertullian.

12 *Service for the Ordering of Deacons.*

13 *Processionale*, 89.

14 *The Clergy and the Catechism*, 108.

15 'Convenient' had a stronger meaning than now in 1662, when it was substituted—doubtless to avoid scandals—for the 'must' of the earlier rubric.

16 The rubric seems clear that the priest's fee is for him who actually solemnises the marriage, and not for the vicar of the parish.

17 The practice of folding the ends of the stole over the hands is of doubtful authority even in the Roman Church. 'There seems no evidence that it was ever done in England.' (Dr. Wickham Legg in *S.P.E.S. Trans.* iii. 169.)

18 Wilkins's *Concilia*, i. 579.

19 In pictures mentioned by Mr Sancroft Randall in his *Ceremonial Connected with the Burial of the Dead* (Church Printing Co.), the following colours occur:—blue copes, blue copes and one purple, bright red and blue copes, black chasuble but one cantor in black copes doubled blue, and the others in blue powdered with gold, cloth of gold chasuble, red curtains to altar and bare altar, blue frontal with gold frontlet. In Mr. St. John Hope's Inventories (*S.P.E.S. Trans.* ii.) the following funeral colours, mostly of chasubles, sets of vestments, and copes, occur:—25 of black, 6 of blue, 3 of purple, 1 of 'violet,' 2 of green, 2 of white.

20 One of Cosin's MS. articles (1627) enquires,—'Whether doth your Minister burie the dead according to the fulle forme, manner, and rites, prescribed in the Book, meeting the corps at the Church-stile, and in his Surplice?'

21 It appears from old pictures that anciently the clergy and servers stood at the side of the grave in no set order.

22 It is worth while mentioning again that the Clergy and Artists Association will put one in touch with artists, craftsmen, and architects for every kind of Church work. The Association makes no charge for advice, and has no financial interest whatever in the work that is done through it.

23 Robertson *On the Liturgy*, 257-8. *Book of Church Law*, 162.

24 In 1605 the 'Cheque-Book' of the Chapel Royal tells us that at the Churching of the Queen, the service was taken by 'the Bishop of Canterbury, being assisted by Mr. Deane of the Chappell (and both in rich copes).'

25 See for this and other interesting matter, Mr. Baden Powell's *Procession in Christian Worship*.

26 *Missale Sarum*, 35. See also the *Consuetudinary* (Frere, 58, 302-4, etc.), and the *Processionale*.

27 See Baden Powell, 12. Also for some useful hints as to out-door processions in country places, 11-12, and as to music, 17-18.

28 Canon 45 orders one sermon every Sunday.

29 The use of the surplice in the pulpit was common in Queen Anne's reign, when it was regarded as a mark of high-churchmanship (Abbey and Overton, ii. 468). But a century or so earlier the gown was also looked upon as a mark of the beast; *e.g.* see some of the Requests to Convocation of 1562, 'that the ministers be not compelled to wear such gowns and caps as the enemies of Christ's gospel have chosen to be the special array of their priesthood.' (Robertson, 92.)

30 Robertson, 103.

31 There are forms of the Bidding Prayer, not only in fifteenth century missals and manuals, but as far back as Leofric's

sacramentary of the tenth century; some of these are given by Dr. Henderson in his edition of the *York Manual* (Surtees Society).

32 Cartwright, the founder of systematic Puritanism, was the first to give up the Bidding Prayer, according to Bishop Wren in his *Parentalia* (p. 90), on the authority of Andrewes and others.

33 But the form in the Sarum Missal, 'Let us pray for the English Church,' is more terse. It begins (*in lingua materna*), '*Oremus pro Ecclcsia Anglicana et pro rege nostro et archiepiscopis episcopis et specialiter pro episcopo nostro N.*'

34 Robertson, 159.

CHAPTER VIII
NOTES ON THE SEASONS

The notes in this chapter are only intended to supplement the directions given in a good calendar, and the remarks as to variations in the service given in other chapters of this book. Consequently, where there is nothing special to be said about a day, I have omitted all mention of it.

For other information the reader is referred to a good Calendar. Dr. Wickham Legg's *Churchman's Oxford Calendar* (Mowbray, 1s.) should be hung in the vestry; and those large churches which may care to follow the old Salisbury use as to lights will find the number for each day specified in Letts's Calendar. Many of the calendars put forth are misleading. Office-hymns are given in Dr. Legg's Calendar, as well as the lessons, colours, and many useful and reliable notes: a small penny Calendar on the same lines is also published by Mowbray, with the lessons and colours.

The Prayer Book Calendar should be loyally followed. There is something, however, to be said for the following additional feasts:— The Falling Asleep of the Blessed Virgin, and All Souls' Day, appear in English almanacks, bearing the *imprimatur* of the Archbishop of Canterbury, down to 1832. The former was erased by Henry VIII. before the Reformation, and without the authority of the Church. The Martyrdom and Translation of St. Thomas of Canterbury were similarly erased, and for obvious reasons.

During Advent and also during Lent the sacred ministers and the clerk should not wear dalmatic or tunicle; for although there is ample evidence that this was sometimes done, the weight of authority[1] is against it. The use of the folded chasuble is too intricate to be dealt with here. The tendency at the present day to make another Lent of Advent is quite modern. The *O Sapientia* in our Calendar may remind us of the spirit of joyful expectation which is the liturgical characteristic of Advent.

Christmas Eve. The eves of the great feasts are generally given up to decorating the church. Solemn Evensong is a fitting preparation for the next day, and a convenient way of imposing a term to the work of decoration. For this service the violet of the vigil will be changed for the festival white. Care should be taken that this service does not interfere with the opportunities of those who wish to make their confessions. A paper on the notice-board, giving the hours at which the clergy can be seen and their initials, will be a great help to timid people; and the clergy should put on their surplices and stoles,[2] and sit in readiness at such hours. The form for giving absolution after private confession is provided by the Prayer Book in the office for the visitation of the sick. This form must be intended to be used at other occasions; for no other is provided for those who seek absolution in response to the Exhortation in the Communion Office. The 113th Canon charges the clergy to keep rigidly the seal of confession.

The decoration of the church with boughs of green stuff has come down to us from the Middle Ages; until the revival it had become generally obsolete except at Christmas. The medieval custom of strewing sweet-smelling herbs on the pavement also lasted long after the Reformation. Holly and mistletoe have been long used at Christmas; but it is a pity that rosemary is forgotten. It was used in honour of the Lord's Mother, and at the time of the *Spectator* and of Gay, and even later,[3] it was still kept up.

A pretty medieval practice was to hang a wooden hoop with candles on it in the midst of the chancel at Christmas in memory of the Star. This was called the Rowell, and it is a good way of marking the season.

The parson will often have to use his authority to protect the altar from childish attempts at over-decoration. In the rest of the church it does not matter so much, and he had perhaps better not interfere, beyond forbidding absolutely the driving in of nails, and the encumbering of altar-rails, stalls, font, or pulpit. But if he do not look after the altar, it will lose its dignity under the inroads of a multitude of good people who do not know what an altar is. Flower-vases are of doubtful legality with us; at all events they should be used sparingly. Decorations should be restrained, following the broad architectural lines of the building. Festoons and wreaths are generally best; and artificial materials are to be avoided. Lettering is one of the most difficult branches of design: it may be remembered that a text is not the more sacred for being illegible.[4] The greenery may in accordance with old custom remain up till the Epiphany (Twelfth Day); or its Octave Day, or Candlemas eve; but the flowers should all be removed on the morrow. Decaying vegetable matter in church is very objectionable. Great reverence and quietness must be observed.

It will be well if the choir sing carols in the streets on Christmas Eve, properly dressed—so long as this does not interfere with the singing at the Midnight Mass. All the parish will be pleased at out-door processions of this kind, and will learn to value others.

Christmas. According to the old custom, there should be three Communions on Christmas Day, the first at midnight, the second at daybreak. The midnight Mass generally attracts many strangers; therefore it is well to insist on intending communicants giving their names to the clergy the day before. Care should be taken that there is one very early Celebration on all the great feasts, for the benefit of servants and others. The more Celebrations there are on these days, the more communicants there will be.

It is an old custom for every one to kneel at the words 'The Word was made Flesh' in the Gospel for the Day.

There seems to be no good reason why carols should be sung at the end of service as a sort of dull afterthought. Without supplanting the Christmas hymns, they may be sung one or two at a time, during the service. Some of them make excellent processionals, others can be sung during the Ablutions, or before and after the Sermon at Evensong, while the more elaborate may be rendered during the Offertory; and this may be continued into the next month with the Epiphany carols. Those who have tried this plan will know how beautiful and stirring is the effect; and the carols teach the people a good deal that our modern hymns fail to teach. As far as legality goes, hymns like carols owe their position in our services solely to custom.

Candlemas. Both the name and the ceremonies were long continued in England. Dr. Donne (d. 1631) in his Sermons[5] defends the 'solemnising' of this day by admitting 'candles into the church,' 'because he who was the light of the world was brought into the temple' on 'this day of lights.' It was still a 'grand Day' at the Temple Church ninety years later;[6] and 'at Ripon, as late as 1790, on the Sunday before Candlemas Day, the Collegiate Church was one continued blaze of light all the afternoon, by reason of an immense number of candles.'[7]

The candles should be blessed before the principal Eucharist of the day. Before the procession they should be distributed by the priest to the other clergy and officials, and, if it is desired, to the people, who hold them lighted during the procession, gospel, and consecration.

The *Benedicite* is generally sung at Mattins from Septuagesima till Easter.

Ash Wednesday is now with us the 'first day of Lent,' and the collect for Ash Wednesday must be said 'every day in Lent,'[8] after the other appointed collect. But no other change is made till the end of the week.

The order of service for Ash Wednesday is as follows:—First Mattins is said in the choir as usual, then the priest goes to faldstool and says the Litany. Then 'after Morning Prayer, the Litany ended according to the accustomed manner, the Priest shall, in the Reading-Pew or Pulpit say' the Commination Service to the end of the Exhortation. For the *Miserere* the priest leaves the pulpit and goes to the faldstool 'in the place where they are accustomed to say the Litany', and 'all kneel upon their knees.' The clerks are told to kneel in the same place as the priests; therefore, if the faldstool be in the middle alley, all will group around it. The impressiveness of this service is often marred by a neglect of the rubrics: the priest should go from stall to faldstool, from faldstool to pulpit, and finally all kneel around the faldstool.

The priest will continue to kneel for the versicles and collects,[9] and for '*Turn thou us*,' which all say together, and he will remain kneeling for the benedictory prayer at the end.

Lent. The Lenten array should be hung up on the Saturday afternoon, or else after Evensong on the first Sunday in Lent.[10] English tradition does not allow of a change of veils for Passiontide, but the same set remain up throughout.

The veils were hung up before the crosses, pictures, and such images as were not of an architectural character, and, where there was a triptych, or other reredos with doors, it was closed. If the reredos has no doors it would be covered by a large veil. The veils were of linen, canvas, fustian, or silk, not of crape; and their colour varied, the most general colours being white or blue.

There is a tendency just now to insist upon white as the colour for Lent veils. This is a mistake:[11] there was a great diversity in old times; blue occurs very frequently, and also red and green.[12] I would suggest that great care is needed in the choice of veils, and that an expert should be consulted; darker colours are safer, as it is very easy to make a church look queer and garish with white, and in my opinion common blue linen generally looks best, and gives the desired impression most clearly to present-day congregations.

It may be mentioned here that very good coloured linens can be got from Harris and Son, Derwent Mills, Cockermouth (but their two or three so-called 'church' colours need not be used). The Ruskin linens are much more expensive, being hand-woven, but they have the beautiful colours and surface of silk: they can be got from Miss Twelves, The Ruskin Linen Industry, Keswick.

The veils were decorated with sacred devices of various kinds, generally in red; sometimes these were pictures in outline. If designed by a competent person, and executed on broad lines, they may be very beautiful and impressive.

A special processional cross was usually reserved for Lent.

In old times it was the custom to omit the *Gloria in Excelsis* in Advent, and from Septuagesima to the end of Lent, and this would no doubt have also been done by those who first used the Prayer Book.

It is a good custom, and based upon ancient practice, to sing during Lent the *Miserere* (Ps. li.) after Evensong, the priest kneeling at the faldstool and singing alternate verses with the people, all kneeling.

Passiontide begins with the 5th Sunday (Passion Sunday). In accordance with old custom, red should be worn, in honour of the Precious Blood; and this, the most solemn season of the year, marked off from the rest of Lent.

Holy Week. The services for Holy Week were of old many and elaborate. The almost universal tendency to supplement those given in the Prayer Book—sometimes by new services, such as the Three Hours, or dissolving views and hymns, sometimes by old, such as the Reproaches or Tenebrae—shows that there is a keen want of more observances during this solemn week.

In using such services, when permission is obtained, we must have at least as much right to follow on the old lines as to adopt new ones. Considering the opposition under which our Prayer Book was compiled, it gives a remarkable amount of space to Holy Week, contains significant references to the ancient services, sometimes in translation, as in the Good Friday Solemn Collects, sometimes in references, as that to Baptism in the Collect for Easter Even. Again, the Church and Court have shown by the Maundy ceremonies that omission of old things does not necessarily mean prohibition.

Those who wish to study the full rites for Holy Week, as they were anciently observed in a great Cathedral, can find them in an *Altar Book* published by Rivington and Percival, and in the *Services for Holy Week* (S.S.O., Waterlow, now out of print). Of course the services of the great cathedrals were much modified in lesser churches.

Palm Sunday, the first day of Holy Week, should be specially observed. The procession of 'palms' is as old as the fourth century, but the introduction of the Blessed Sacrament into the Procession was of course much later; possibly it was due in this country to Lanfranc. Anciently every village had at least its procession of palms.

The dried date-palms often used are an innovation, and the appropriateness of using bleached and dead leaves of this kind may well be questioned. If they are used at all, the ancient 'flowers and branches' should be used as well. Willow and yew, for instance, look much better on the altar than the long palms which one often sees propped in awkward curves against the reredos. The word 'palm' was anciently applied to willow and yew indifferently;[13] and their use, at least out of church, has never been dropped in this country. Box and flowers were also used.

The procession takes place before the Eucharist only, and not at Evensong. Before the procession, the veils of the altar-cross (both on the high-altar and on minor altars) should be untied so that they can be easily removed. The palms for distribution should be placed on a tray by the south side of the altar, the palms for the ministers on the altar itself.

The priest, wearing a red cope over his albe, etc., enters the sanctuary with the ministers (who do not wear their dalmatics) as usual. He first blesses the palms; more anciently the blessing was very short; but in the Sarum Missal it has become a long service, with collects, lesson, and gospel. There may be no objection to the lesson and gospel being read, if it is desired. The lesson (read by the clerk on the epistle side) is Exodus xv. 27-xvi. 10; the gospel (read by a deacon on the gospel side) is John xii. 12-19. The palms are blessed after the gospel.

After the palms have been distributed to the ministers and choir (and for this I would suggest bunches of willow), the distribution to the people commences. During it a hymn may be sung, or permission could no doubt be obtained for the ancient anthems.

If there is only a clerk to assist, he will carry the palms to the chancel-gate and supply them to the priest: if there is a deacon he will take this office, and then the clerk will hold up the border of the priest's cope. The verger had best stand with his. wand in the middle alley, and see that the people come two and two up the middle, and go back by the side alleys. They should kneel as they take the palms.

The distribution ended, all will join in the procession, carrying their palms and singing *Gloria laus et honor* (98). The procession will go the usual way, by the left. The Gospel for the first Sunday in Advent may be sung as a station on the south side of the church.

After the procession is over, the clerk unveils the altar-cross, and the Eucharist proceeds as usual. All bow profoundly, and a short pause is made, at the words *'yielded up the Ghost'* in the Gospel, both now and on the following days. The altar-cross is veiled again after Evensong.

On the Wednesday, Thursday, and Friday of Holy Week the ancient office of Tenebrae may be said.

Permission is readily given for this service, as it consists entirely of passages from Holy Scripture with the addition of a few readings from St. Augustine. The English office of Tenebrae is published by J. T. Hayes, 17 Henrietta Street, Covent Garden, under the name of *English Tenebrae*. The service in this, the most correct edition, is printed in full each day, so that there is no trouble about finding the place. Tenebrae should be sung, without the organ; but in some places it may be found more convenient to monotone it, or to sing the *Benedictus* at the end only.

The service is held in the evening. There should only be enough light for people to read by. The verger and churchwardens should be ready to supply copies of English Tenebrae.

The Tenebrae candlestick or 'herse,' with its twenty-four candles, should be placed before the altar on the epistle side, and lighted before the service begins.

The Psalms are sung without the *Gloria*. A candle is extinguished at each antiphon and at each of the responsories which follow the Lessons, by a server appointed for this office: in his book the number of the candle should be written plainly against each antiphon and responsory. He will begin with the lowest candle, first on one side, then on the next, and so on. All may sit: the service is long, especially if it be sung. The lectern should stand in the midst of the choir, and he who is to read leaves his stall before each set of lessons[14] to do so.

During the last psalm before the *Benedictus*, the upper light is removed, and put in some place where it is not seen, but is not extinguished. The lights in the church should then be lowered as much as possible. After the Good Friday collect has been said, 'one of the servers striking his book with his hand three times, all shall rise and the lighted candle shall be brought forth,' and put on the herse. All go out silently, and the candle is extinguished after the service.

Maundy-Thursday, the Birthday of the Eucharist as it was well called, was also most appropriately the day of the Reconciliation of Penitents, in accordance with that 'godly discipline'[15] which our Prayer Book recommends. From the fifth century the ceremony of consecrating the Chrism was fixed for this day also; but in the West this office has been from an early period restricted to Bishops. The very early ceremony of washing the feet of twelve or thirteen poor men was also confined to bishops and other great ecclesiastical and secular personages. Cranmer practised and defended the custom. Queen Elizabeth kept it up, herself washing and kissing the feet of as many poor persons as corresponded with her age. The Hanoverian sovereigns deputed the office to the royal almoners, who soon dropped the washing, but retained the custom of giving alms, which is still done in church with some ceremony each year. It is to this practice that we owe the name of Maundy.

The Holy Eucharist should be sung with much solemnity on this its birthday. The colour may be white for the Holy Eucharist. Dalmatics and tunicles are worn. The *Agnus Dei* should not be sung, unless the Bishop celebrates.

Evensong was anciently said directly after the Eucharist, and then the altars were stripped and washed, priests, ministers, and torchbearers all vested in albes, while two boys carried wine and water. Each altar was washed, wine and then water being poured on its five crosses, then dried with a branch of box, and the collect said for the saint in whose honour the altar was dedicated. Meanwhile responsories were sung. It is a reasonable and useful as well as symbolical custom to wash the altars on this day;[16] they should remain stripped till Easter Eve. The altar was only vested on Good Friday during the Mass of the Presanctified.

All the church bells should be silent during the last three days of Holy Week after the Maundy Mass. Therefore we have no precedent for the objectionable and morbid practice of tolling a bell on Good Friday.

Good Friday. The services essential to this day are Mattins, Litany, the Ante-Communion service, and Evensong. To these may be added the Reproaches in the morning and Tenebrae after Evensong, if permission has been obtained from the Ordinary. The Three Hours' Service is everywhere allowed, and many find it a very great help. It is not, however, a liturgical service at all; and, excellent as revivalist devotions of this kind often are, they must not be allowed to displace the Church's appointed offices.

The service sometimes used, called the 'Reproaches,' is really a small part of the old office for the Veneration of the Cross, and so is the hymn *Pange Lingua* (A. and M. 97).

The Holy Eucharist should not be celebrated on Good Friday.

The Passiontide red should be continued (unless the violet is kept on, in which case the colour may be violet or black). There is no authority for the use of black crape, etc., in the church.

Anciently, three Hosts were consecrated on Maundy-Thursday: the second was consumed by the priest at the Mass of the Presanctified (of which the custom of using the Ante-Communion office is a representation), the third Host was deposited in the Easter Sepulchre, which was not the same thing as the urn on the Roman 'altar of repose.'

The most practicable arrangement at an ordinary town church will probably be something like this:— At 9.30 a.m., service for children with several quite short addresses and a few hymns; at 10, Mattins, Litany, Ante-Communion service; at 12, perhaps, the Three Hours' devotion; at 6, Evensong; and at 8, Tenebrae, opportunity being given after the Three Hours, Evensong, and Tenebrae for those who seek the ministry of reconciliation.

Mattins and Litany having been said without note, the priest will go to the altar and say the Ante-Communion service, as it is appointed in the Prayer Book. The choir might sing the Tract Psalm cxl. As there is no Communion with the presanctified Host, the altar will not be vested but will remain stripped. For the same reason the priest will not wear a chasuble, but will vest as for the Ante-Communion service in the First Prayer Book,[17] 'a plain albe or surplice, with a cope.' The cope will be red (unless the Passiontide colour is not used), and neither priest nor ministers will wear apparels on their albes or amices.

The great feature of the old service was intercession, and some of the solemn collects then used have been preserved in our service. The intercessions were for the King, bishops and clergy, confessors and all 'the holy people of God,' those in heresy or schism, the Jews and the heathen, the troubles and sickness in the world, and the catechumens. Our collects preserve most of these subjects; and perhaps in addition to those appointed, *i.e.* for the Queen, 'this thy family,' 'all estates of men in thy holy Church,' 'all Jews, Turks, Infidels, and Hereticks' and the Ash Wednesday collect, one or two of the collects at the end of the Communion service might be added, in accordance with the rubric, *e.g. 'Assist us,'* and the second, or fifth.

After the Church Militant Prayer one or more of the collects at the end of the service will be said, as the rubric directs. The most suitable for the occasion is the last, *'Almighty God, who hast promised.'*

At the end of the old service, the priest and ministers went out in order, but the rest remained to say their private prayers, and departed without set order.

If the Three Hours' Devotion be observed, the preacher might wear his cassock and gown, as he would at a mission-service, and not a surplice. He will not wear a stole.

Evensong was anciently said 'without note.'

Easter Even, the Great Sabbath, or Holy Saturday, was anciently marked by the blessing of the new fire and the Paschal candle, and by the hallowing of the Font. The Collect for the Day makes special allusion to its connection with Holy Baptism. It is a good occasion for holding a Solemn Baptism, and when adults seek admission to the Church their baptism should, when it is convenient, be fixed for this day.

There should be no solemn Evensong on Easter Eve. The crosses may be unveiled in the evening.

The question as to whether there should be a Mass on Easter Even has been much disputed. Anciently the Mass was not till midnight. In any case it seems to be agreed on all hands that there should be no consecration till after mid-day.

In the Sarum Missal, Mass was said on Easter Even after the blessing of the Paschal. More anciently there was no Mass on this day, and the Paschal was blessed in the evening.

The Passiontide red should be used (unless the violet be retained) or else white. The offices in the Prayer Book are Mattins, Communion, and Evensong. The Litany, or a metrical litany, should also be sung, as litanies were a feature of the old services for this day.

Easter is the day on which our Church orders all the faithful to communicate. Every opportunity ought therefore to be given, and the congregation reminded beforehand; and a Celebration held at a very early hour for the benefit of those who cannot come later. It is a good plan to have sheets of foolscap on a table near the door, in charge of the verger, so that the communicants may enter their names and addresses as they go out.

The Rogation Days should be carefully kept as days of intercession for God's blessing on the fruits of the earth. The Litany should be said before the principal Eucharist on each day, violet being the colour for these two services. The late Archbishop of Canterbury, in urging the better observance of these days, sanctioned two special collects which may be obtained from the S.P.C.K.; an epistle and gospel is provided in Canon Carter's book. The Archbishop also recommended the substitution of Psalms lxv., lxvi., and lxvii. for the Psalms of the day, 'and the use of the Litany at some hour on the Monday and Tuesday, as well as on Sunday and Wednesday.'

Archbishop Benson also urged that, 'Where the Perambulation of Parish Bounds is still observed and suitable, I hope that it will always be with such religious service as is happily used in many places.' Unfortunately the old processions had become associated with tin-cans (both empty and full) and with much unseemliness. But in country places the people welcome a revival of the old religious processions; and the parson who omits them loses a great opportunity of touching and helping his flock. In large towns the case is rather different.

As late as about 1765, at Wolverhampton, 'the sacrist, resident prebendaries, and members of the choir, assembled at Morning

Prayers on Monday and Tuesday in Rogation Week, with the charity children bearing long poles clothed with all kinds of flowers then in season, and which were afterwards carried through the streets of the town with much solemnity, the clergy, singing men and boys, dressed in their sacred vestments, closing the procession, and chanting in a grave and appropriate melody the' *Benedicite*. The boundaries of the parish were marked in many points by Gospel trees, where the Gospel was read.[18]

Here then we touch hands with ancient tradition; and the parson may easily accommodate it to his own opportunities. Something like the following may be found suitable.

Let the choir and clergy leave the church, preceded by the churchwardens,[19] verger, cross, thurifer, and torch- or lantern-bearers, all wearing surplices over their cassocks, and the clergy their hoods, tippets, and caps (the officiant in a violet cope). Let the choir be followed by the school-children carrying flowers and garlands. Let stations be previously arranged, one in the village, the rest on the boundaries if possible (if trees be planted, all the better). Let the choir slowly chant the 67th Psalm[20] through the village; and at the first station let the Gospel for the Sunday be read, the choir grouping round the reader. As the precession proceeds let the Litany be sung, and perhaps metrical litanies, and the Penitential Psalms to fill up the time; and at the other stations let the Epistle and Gospel for the Rogation Days (James v. 16-20 and Luke xi. 5-13) be read, and other passages if there are more stations. On returning through the village by another way let the *Benedicite* be sung.

The parson may be able to arrange for a partial holiday on these occasions.

Ascension Day. Everything should be done to make Holy Thursday as much a holiday as Christmas, and the people strongly urged to observe it according to the custom of Holy Church. It may help towards this ideal if the day is chosen for some guild or club feast.

Whitsuntide (Eve) is a proper occasion for the administration of Solemn Baptism.

The Dedication Festival should be kept on the first Sunday in October with an octave.

All Souls' Day, which follows All Saints' Day, has some authority for its observance. A Eucharist for the repose of the departed[21] might certainly be said on this day; and it may be useful to preach a sermon in the evening. If the people are unprejudiced, they will be grateful for this opportunity of remembering their departed friends.

Ember Days. The Ember Day collects are directed by the rubric after Prayers and Thanksgivings to be said 'before the two final prayers of the Litany, or of Morning and Evening Prayer.' Special forms for the Communion are sanctioned, and can be obtained from the S.P.C.K. There are special post-communions in the Ordination services.

On the Patronal Festival a station may be made, in the procession, before the altar of the patron saint, if there be one, all standing while the collect for the saint is said. Before the collect the priest censes the altar and then says 'Let us pray.'

Notes

1 *Consuetudinary*, 163.

2 The picture in Van der Weyden's Seven Sacraments, however, and the illumination reproduced in Pt. i. of the *Prymer* (E. Eng. Text Soc.) show the priest in absolution, with almuce on head, but without stole.

3 Cf. Abbey and Overton, ii. 452.

4 Simple letters are better than the so-called Gothic types one often sees. Many beautiful examples are given in Mr. E. F. Strange's *Alphabets* (Bell: 5s.).

5 Pp. 80, 112. Cf. *Lincoln Judgement*, 71.

6 Paterson, *Pietas Lond.* 273.

7 Walcot, *Cath.* 199. Cosin also was charged by the Puritans with 'burning two hundred wax candles in one Candlemas night' in Durham Cathedral: they were lit ceremonially by a company of boys, with many bows. *Ibid.* 165. Cosin denied the large number.

8 Some authorities consider that 'every day in Lent' means, as it did in the Sarum Breviary, every day from the first Monday till the Wednesday in Holy Week, excluding Sundays and feast days— 'every day' being merely a translation of 'ferial.' But it seems safer to take the words literally, as has been the custom.

9 These being from the Sarum Missal *Benedictio Cinerum* (Burntisland Ed., p. 131), where kneeling for the versicles and collects, is directed.

10 *Consuetudinary*, i. 101. Saturday is more convenient, and has sufficient precedent.

11 Blue must have been most usual at the time of our Rubric; for in the *Beehive of the Romish Church*, 1580 (fo. 190 b.) we read—'The whole of Lent they doe cause their images to looke through a blewe cloth.'

12 *E.g.* Holy Week Cer. 44-7. *S.P.E.S. Trans.* ii. 244.

13 It still is in the vernacular; and there can be no more striking; instance of the persistence of old customs than the sight of the costers' barrows in London streets on the Saturday evening before Palm Sunday, where catkin willow and box are freely sold.

14 Cranmer explained that the Lamentations are read in memory of the Jews seeking our Lord's life at this time.

15 'In the Primitive Church there was a godly discipline, that, at the beginning of Lent, such persons as stood convicted of notorious sin were put to open penance...(until the said discipline may be restored again, which is much to be wished).'—*Introduction of the Commination Service*.

Yet Church Discipline was, even throughout the eighteenth century, a much greater reality than at the present day. Excommunications and presentments were still in force, and the commutation of penance was a matter of grave and careful consideration even by so strong a Protestant as William III. Wordsworth has told us that one of his earliest recollections (about 1777) was seeing a woman doing penance in a white sheet: this was called 'solemn penance.' Bishop Wilson's remarkable system of discipline can be read in his life. (Cf. Abbey and Overton, ii. 499-511.) Discipline was vigorously enforced by the Presbyterians during their ascendency in England. It is still in force in the ecclesiastical courts in the case of slander.

16 It is absolutely necessary that the altars should be sometimes, washed and left bare to be aired.

17 Chapter III.

18 Brand's *Popular Antiquities*, i. 169.

19 At first staves were carried, then rods or wands *ad defendendum. processionem* (Chambers, 213). Four stalwart men in their ordinary attire, carrying rods, would make a good head to the procession.

20 The ancient practice was to sing Ps. lxvii. (and any other psalms for any special need, such as good weather or peace), and Litanies, filling up with the Penitential Psalms (Chambers, 211). Elizabeth's injunctions ordered Ps. ciii. and civ. to be sung in the perambulation.

21 With the Burial Service Collect, '*Almighty God with whom,*' and the epistle and gospel 1 Thess. iv. 13 to end, and John xi. 21-28.

LIST OF BOOKS
REFERRED TO IN THE FOREGOING PAGES

Abbey and Overton. *The English Church in the Eighteenth Century.* 2 vols. Longmans. 1878.

Archbishop of Canterbury's Court. *Read and Others* v. *the Lord Bishop of Lincoln, Judgement,* 1890. Macmillans. 1894.

Barnes, Rev. A. S. *Low Mass in England before the Reformation.* Church Printing Company. 1892.

Barry, Bishop Alfred. *Teachers' Prayer Book.* Queen's Printers.

Blunt, Rev. J. H. *Annotated Book of Common Prayer.* Rivingtons. 1866.

Blunt and Phillimore. *The Book of Church Law.* 8th ed. Longmans. 1899.

Brand, J. *Popular Antiquities.* Ed. Ellis. 1813.

Bridgett, Rev. T. E. *History of the Holy Eucharist in Great Britain.* 2 vols. Kegan Paul. 1881.

Cardwell, Ed. *A History of Conferences connected with the Revision of the Book of Common Prayer.* Oxford. 1840.

Cardwell, Ed. *Documentary Annals.* 2 vols. Oxford. 1839.

Carter, Rev. T. T. *Collects, Epistles, and Gospels for certain Occasions and Holy Days.* Masters. 1882.

Chambers, J. D. *Divine Worship in England.* Pickering. 1877.

Collier, Jeremy. *Ecclesiastical History of Great Britain.* 2 vols. fol. London. 1714.

Constitutions and Canons Ecclesiastical. S.P.C.K. 1894.

Consuetudinary. See Register of St. Osmund.

Consuetudinary (Frere). See Frere, Rev. W. H.

Cookson, James. *Family Prayer Book and Companion to the Altar.* 3rd ed. Winchester. 1789.

Duchesne, L. *Origines du Culte Chrétien.* 2nd ed. Paris. 1898.

Low, Sidney J., and F. S. Pulling. *Dictionary of English History*. Cassell. 1884.

Dixon, Canon R. W. *History of the Church of England*. Routledge. 1881.

Donne, Dr. J. *LXXX. Sermons*. fol. 1640.

Feasey, H. J. *Ancient English Holy Week Ceremonial*. T. Baker. 1897.

First Prayer Book of Edward VI., 1549. 8th thous. Parker. 1887.

Frere, Rev. W. H. *The Use of Sarum I. The Sarum Customs as set forth in the Consuetudinary and Customary*. Cambridge Univ. Press. 1898.

Gardiner, S. R. *Student's History of England.*

Gasquet, Dom F. A., and E. Bishop. *Edward VI. and the Book of Common Prayer*. Hodges. 1890.

Grindal, Archbishop, *Remains of*. Parker Soc., Cambridge. 1843.

Heylyn, Peter. *Antidotum Lincolniense*. London. 1637.

Hierurgia Anglicana. Edited by members of the Ecclesiological Society. Rivingtons. 1848.

Isherwood, Rev. W. S. *Altar Lights and Classification of Feasts* (Society of St. Osmund, vol. i.). Church Printing Company.

Johnson, John. *The Clergyman's Vade Mecum*. 6th ed. 2 vols. London. 1731.

Jones, Rev. Spencer. *The Clergy and the Catechism*. 6th ed. Skeffington. 1897.

Kempe, Rev. J. W. *Reservation of the Blessed Sacrament*. Palmer. 1887.

Lacey, Rev. T. A. *Liturgical Interpolations* (Alcuin Club). Longmans. 1898.

Leslie, Charles. *Theological Works*. 7 vols. Oxford. 1832.

Maskell, William. *The Ancient Liturgy of the Church of England*. Pickering. 1844.

Micklethwaite, J. T. *The Ornaments of the Rubric* (Alcuin Club). Longmans. 1897.

Missale Sarum. Burntisland ed. Parker. 1861-83.

Notes on Ceremonial. Pickering. 3rd ed., 1888.

Overton, Rev. J. H. *The Church in England*. 2 vols. Wells, Gardner. 1898.

Paterson, James. *Pietas Londinensis*. 1714.

Perry, Rev. T. W. *Lawful Church Ornaments*. Masters. 1857.

Perry, Rev. T. W. *Notes on the Judgement of the Jud. Committee of the Privy Council, Hibbert v. Purchas*. Masters. 1877.

Powell, Rev. J. Baden. *The Procession in Christian Worship*. English Church Union.

Processionale ad Usum Sarum. M'Corquodale. 1882.

Randall, W. Sancroft. *Ceremonial and offices connected with the Burial of the Dead* (Society of St. Osmund). Church Printing Company.

Record Office. Inventory quoted from *Beckenham in the Olden Times*. Miss C. A. N. Trollope. Beckenham. Thornton. 1898.

Register of St. Osmund, Ed. W. H. Rich Jones. (Rolls Series.) Longmans. 1883.

Robertson, Professor J. Craigie. *How shall we Conform to the Liturgy*. 3rd ed. Murray. 1869.

St. Paul's Ecclesiological Society, Transactions of (quoted as *S.P.E.S. Trans.*) 4 vols. Alabaster, Passmore. Harrison and Sons. 1881-1898.

Sarum Missal in English. Ed. A. H. Pearson. 2nd ed. Church Printing Company. 1884.

Services of Holy Week from the Sarum Missal. Society of St. Osmund. Waterlow. 1895.

Scobell, Henry. *Collection of Acts in the Parliaments...1640...1656*. fol. London. 1658.

Strype, John. *Memorials of Cranmer*. New ed. P. E. Barnes. 2 vols. Routledge. 1853.

Wakeman, H. Offley. *An Introduction to the History of the Church of England*. 3rd ed. Rivingtons. 1897.

Walcott, Mackenzie E. C. *Traditions and Customs of Cathedrals*. 2nd ed. Longmans. 1872.

Wilkins. *Concilia Mag. Brittannia.e* 4 vols. fol. London, 1737.

Wilson, Bishop Thos., *Life of*, by J. Keble. *Works*, vol. i. (Angl. Cath. Lib.). Parker. 1863.

Wren, Christopher. *Parentalia, Memoirs of the Family of the Wrens*, fol. London. 1750.

APPENDIX

The following very brief summary of the Archbishop of York's Pastoral (Dec. 1898) may be of use. The pastoral was delivered after this handbook was in type.

The Bishop's unanimity on these points is absolute. We have to obey the Prayer Book as it is. The daily services should be said. Provision should be made for the holy days and fasts which are in the Prayer Book, but other festivals are not to be observed. No ceremony to be introduced that is not 'clearly authorised or sanctioned by the Prayer Book'; but hymns are an exception to this rule. The Ornaments Rubric not to be obeyed without the Bishop's sanction. 'The ceremonial use of incense as in the censing of persons and things cannot be sanctioned'; but its still use might be tolerated. The sprinkling of water cannot be sanctioned. Pictures and images may be allowed, but not the placing of candles before them. Reservation must be wholly discontinued; though in special cases of emergency 'permission might possibly be given to carry the Holy Communion directly' from the service in church, without any reservation. There is no authority for the omission of the Commandments, or of Collect, Epistle, and Gospel. All additions to the service are equally inadmissible ; 'for example the ringing of a bell at the moment of consecration, either within or outside of the church.' To celebrate the Holy Communion 'in a choral form with everything that can add to its dignity and solemnity' is in every way allowable; but there must be persons present to partake of the Holy Sacrament, and there must be 'an open and evident readiness' to receive communicants. No additional service may be introduced without the Bishop's sanction first obtained. Interpolations are inadmissible. Invocations cannot be allowed, 'nor definite prayers for the dead.' The Church of England does not allow confession to be made compulsory.